THE IMMORTAL 600

Surviving Civil War Charleston and Savannah

D1520803

KAREN STOKES

Charleston London

THE
History
PRESS

Published by The History Press
Charleston, SC 29403
www.historypress.net

Copyright © 2013 by Karen Stokes
All rights reserved

Front cover: Burial at Fort Pulaski. Painting by Martin Pate, Newnan, Georgia. *Courtesy of Southeastern Archeological Center, NPS.*

First published 2013

Manufactured in the United States

ISBN 978.1.60949.989.1

Library of Congress CIP data applied for.

Contents

Acknowledgements

The author is once again indebted to the South Carolina Historical Society for the use of its wonderful manuscript, book and visual material collections, and to author Mike Coker, who offered encouragement and helpful advice about the book, including the title. Special thanks are also due to R. Hugh Simmons of the Fort Delaware Society, who possesses a wealth of factual knowledge about the Fort Delaware prison camp and whose personal observations and suggestions about the book only served to improve it.

Introduction

This is the story of a remarkable group of men who endured injustice and cruelty as prisoners of the United States government during the war that raged in America from 1861 to 1865. Six hundred prisoners of war, all Confederate officers, were chosen to undergo an extraordinary ordeal that would earn them a place in history as "The Immortal 600." Most of them were held as "human shields" on an island in the harbor of Charleston, South Carolina, surviving a fearful barrage of artillery fire from nearby Confederate forts and batteries, and then, at Fort Pulaski near Savannah, Georgia, others were subjected to an even more appalling ordeal—but the story of the six hundred begins at Fort Delaware, a Federal prisoner of war camp located in the state of Delaware.

In the summer of 1863, a large number of Confederate prisoners from Gettysburg and Vicksburg arrived at Fort Delaware, significantly increasing the prison population. Before this time in the war, many of these soldiers would have enjoyed a good chance of exchange. Although attended with many controversies between the two governments, the exchange of prisoners of war between the United States and the Confederacy had been going on under the articles of the Dix-Hill Cartel since its enactment in July 1862. Less than a year later, however, the United States government put a stop to most prisoner exchanges, and after this, many thousands of men held in prisons in the North and South languished and died in captivity.

In 1864, in response to allegations of deliberate mistreatment of Union prisoners by their Confederate captors, the Union authorities commenced a policy of retaliation against prisoners of war in their hands. The retaliatory measures included reducing the food rations of Confederate prisoners and restricting their receipt of food and other comforts sent into prisons from family and friends. As a result, there was a rise in malnourishment, as well as all the sufferings and afflictions that went along with it, among the prisoners held by the North. The most singular and unconscionable manifestation of this retaliatory policy occurred when six hundred captive Confederate officers were taken out of Fort Delaware and sent into harsh, sometimes hellish conditions at Union prisons in South Carolina and Georgia.

CHAPTER 1

Prisoners of War at Fort Delaware

Fort Delaware was constructed in the 1850s on a marshy island, or rather a mud shoal, called Pea Patch Island, in the middle of the Delaware River. A massive pentagonal structure of granite and brick, it was surrounded by a wide moat. The walls of the fort enclosed a large parade ground, and 156 guns were mounted in its casemates, guarding both sides of the river. The acreage of the island had been reclaimed from swamplands by the building of levees, and when it rained sufficiently, the loamy, spongy soil became an unhealthy quagmire of mud and filth.

The fort was adapted for use as a prison in the early years of the War Between the States. Inside its walls, some of the windowed chambers for the guns (casemates) were floored to be used as prison cells, and outside, wooden sheds were constructed to accommodate the growing number of prisoners of war. Rooms in the garrison barracks inside the fort were set aside for Confederate officers of higher rank and other prisoners. In the spring of 1863, an expanded complex of wooden barracks was begun outside the fort on Pea Patch Island to house ten thousand prisoners. A six-hundred-bed hospital was also built outside the fort on the north end of the island adjacent to the new prison barracks. The barracks were barely complete when the first wave of Confederate prisoners began to arrive from Gettysburg in July 1863.

The prisoners housed in the new wooden barracks were grouped in administrative "divisions" numbering up to one hundred men. The

Fort Delaware, located on Pea Patch Island in the Delaware River. This is one of the illustrations in Reverend Isaac Handy's diary, published in 1874. *From the author's collection.*

enclosed yard, or pen, for the Confederate officers (with a capacity of two thousand) was an area of about two acres containing the barracks and a mess hall. It was surrounded by a high wooden fence and was directly under the guns of the fort. There was a larger adjacent prison pen for the private soldiers (capacity eight thousand), and it was separated from the officers' area by an alley and two plank fences topped by catwalks, where sentries walked and kept watch night and day. A number of drainage ditches ran in all directions across the prison yards. Their brownish-green, nearly stagnant waters, controlled by flood gates, served to float off the waste and offal of thousands of prisoners, sometimes barely adequately.

In July 1864, Captain Henry C. Dickinson, a Confederate prisoner from Virginia, recorded his first impressions of Fort Delaware when he arrived at the island's wharf in a crowded steamboat:

> *A levee is constructed around the whole island, but the spring tides sometimes carry the water over the walls. The officers' gardens, I noticed, were in a high state of cultivation; indeed, they ought to be, being of alluvial soil, and irrigated by the ditches which convey the water into the moat around the fort. The fort walls were of granite or brown stone,*

quadrangular, and built for three tiers of guns. I expect if necessary two hundred guns could be mounted. I counted once about seventy in the western wall, besides twelve large guns on the parapet. The officers' quarters, etc., were within the walls of the fort and made of brick. A bridge with a draw led to the fort on the west side. When we landed...we were marched on a lawn near the hospitals, where we were counted, rolls were called and a full search was made. I hid my money and valuables in the grass till the search was over.

In addition to prisoners of war, there were also a number of political prisoners held at Fort Delaware. After the war began, President Abraham Lincoln suspended the writ of habeas corpus (a court order protecting citizens from unlawful detention), and during the course of the conflict, thousands of citizens, mostly Northerners, were arrested and incarcerated in various prisons. One of these political prisoners was Reverend Isaac W.K. Handy, a civilian Presbyterian minister. In the summer of 1863, after Handy made remarks critical of the United States government in a private conversation, he was reported, arrested and, without trial or due process, imprisoned at Fort Delaware. Reverend Handy believed that taking the oath of allegiance to the United States was tantamount to giving approval of the war, and, calling himself "a prisoner for conscience' sake," he refused to yield, although by taking the oath, he could have secured his release. During his fifteen months of confinement, he secretly kept a diary, and after the war, it was published and serves as a useful and reliable source about conditions in the prison, revealing what it was like to be a prisoner there for thousands of Confederate soldiers and officers, including the six hundred men destined to be taken out of Fort Delaware in August 1864.

In May 1864, Reverend Handy was moved into the wooden barracks of the Confederate officers, but before then, for nearly a year, he resided with the other political prisoners and Confederate officers who were quartered within the walls of the fort. These captives were better off for food and shelter than many of the other prisoners. On August 4, 1863, the clergyman described an incident that illustrated the difference between the treatment of those inside the fort and some of the prisoners kept outside its walls:

A number of prisoners came into the Fort-yard this morning, to get water, and to remove some bedding. Several of them crowding into a recess, out

Above: Reverend Isaac W.K. Handy, a Presbyterian minister, secretly kept a diary during his fifteen months of confinement at Fort Delaware as a political prisoner. *From the author's collection.*

Opposite: This illustration from Reverend Handy's diary depicts an incident in which he observed hungry Confederate prisoners catching crusts of bread tossed out to them from other prisoners inside the fort. *From the author's collection.*

of sight of the sentinels, we soon found that the poor fellows were suffering for food, and two or three of our party threw them something to eat. The supply of bread, in all the rooms, seemed tolerably full, and we succeeded in getting a dozen or more loaves, which were thrown out to the sufferers in halves and quarters. It distressed me, to see the eagerness with which they threw up their hands, to catch at every piece.

Although there were many Northern prisons with much higher mortality rates, disease was sometimes rampant at Fort Delaware, and some prisoners suffered from scurvy and dysentery. About half of all the deaths that occurred were due to a smallpox epidemic in 1863. Because of the marshy ground of the island, the bodies of the prisoners were buried in mass graves in nearby New Jersey. The commandant of the fort later claimed in his own defense, "The number of deaths rendered it impossible to dig a grave for each body separately."

Many of the cases of dysentery in the prison population could likely be traced to unsanitary water. While residing inside the fort in 1863, Reverend Handy wrote it had caused him and other political prisoners to become sick with that condition (though later on, the clergyman reported that the quality of the water provided to the fort prisoners had improved). In September 1864, after being moved outside the fort, Reverend Handy described the water at Fort Delaware as "miserable stuff." There was cleaner water in containers called hogsheads, but the water in the drainage ditches was often filthy. He wrote:

> *The hogsheads afford some little relief for drinking purposes; but the ditches are our only resource for washing in every department. The brackish current which comes in from the bay, is usually covered with a green scum, and infested with insects. Everybody resorts to the banks; and it is common to see men at one end washing dishes; a little farther down, a party scrubbing shirts and handkerchiefs—whilst at the lower end, several persons may be noticed in a state of perfect nudity, trying the effect of a salt bath. Added to this, some one will presently come along with a foul vessel, and throwing the contents into the common reservoir, return to quarters, no man saying aught against him. The only defense against this monstrosity of filth is a comparatively clean wash in the early morning, when the tide has had some little opportunity to carry off the accumulations of the preceding day.*

On Captain Henry C. Dickinson's first day at Fort Delaware as a prisoner of war in 1864, he received a rude surprise when he attempted to bathe himself:

> *My first wish after getting into my quarters was to take a wash, and seeing a great hogshead at [Division] No. 32, I procured a pan and helped myself, but was told, "That hogshead is for drinking; you must wash in the ditch." This ditch is full of salt water, connecting with the main ditch at the officers' sinks [latrines]…and the receptacle of all the loose filth on the island. The water was supposed to be renewed in it by the ebb and flow of the tides, but the numerous "water gaps" made to prevent our escape caught all the scum and filth at the ebb, which was drawn back by the flow, so that the ditch was only cleaned when "Fox," a hideous, hang-dog looking Irishman (who was a deserter from the Stonewall Brigade), scraped out the "settlings" with mud and a hoe. Often, whilst I have been washing my face and hands, have I seen three or four, naked, washing their bodies, others washing their feet, others washing their greasy dishes, others washing handkerchiefs or socks, and others again cleaning catfish and throwing the intestines in the water. All this was done in the same stagnant ditch within a few feet of each other.*

The commanding officer at Fort Delaware, General Albin F. Schoepf, was a European who had immigrated to the United States in 1851. Born

Fort Delaware prisoners washing their clothes and bodies in the stagnant water of the ditches that ran in all directions across the prison pen. *From the author's collection.*

in Poland, he entered a military academy in Austria as a youth and was later commissioned as an officer in the Austrian army. He was serving in Hungary when an uprising occurred there in 1848, and he resigned his commission to join the revolutionaries, but the revolution was soon suppressed, and Schoepf left the country. A few years later, like many of the "Forty-Eighters" who supported or took part in socialist and nationalist revolutionary movements prevalent in Europe at that time, Schoepf came to the United States. He served in several government bureaus including the War Department, and after the war began, he was appointed to the rank of brigadier general in the United States Army. After serving as a field commander, he was transferred to the command of Fort Delaware in April 1863.

There were differing opinions about Schoepf among the Confederate prisoners, who generally believed him to be a Hungarian or a German. Captain Henry C. Dickinson described the commandant as a "fat old Dutchman speaking English badly, by rank a brigadier general and named A. Schoepf, pronounced Sheff." Dickinson added, "So far as administrative ability went he was totally unfitted to command." Robert E. Park, an imprisoned officer of the Twelfth Alabama Infantry Regiment, wrote of him:

Brigadier-General A. Schoepf, a Hungarian, is in command, and has two very unpopular and insolent officers, Captain G.W. Ahl and Lieutenant Woolf, his adjutants. These uniformed plebians delight in exercising petty tyranny over their superiors in the prison. They are rude, coarse men, with no conception of sentiments of generosity and magnanimity. Woolf is generally drunk, boastful and boisterous. Ahl is more genteel in speech and manner, but less obliging, and more cruel. General Schoepf is disposed to be lenient and kind, but is terribly afraid of his superior officers, especially Secretary [of War] *Stanton. He is a moral coward…General Schoepf, the Hungarian, and General Meagher, the Irishman, surely forget the oppressions they pretend to lament in their own native lands, while assisting our enemies to enslave and destroy ours.*

John Ogden Murray, a Confederate officer from Virginia, characterized Schoepf as "a German, in his way a very good sort of an old fellow, who, no doubt, did all he dare do, if report is correct, to alleviate the condition of Confederate prisoners of war." Similarly, in his reminiscences of the war, Colonel Abram Fulkerson of Tennessee described Schoepf as "a humane officer who did all he dared to alleviate the sufferings of the prisoners." Henry C. Dickinson, however, had his doubts about the general and was not convinced that Schoepf was "kindly disposed toward the prisoners." In his diary, Dickinson commented that he had "many reasons to believe that Schoepf was not as good as the most partial represent him, though it is possible that the abuses existed because of a want of system, added to the influence of Ahl."

It appears that many of the prisoners laid much of the blame for any bad treatment at Fort Delaware on Schoepf's despised subordinate officers, Captain George W. Ahl and Lieutenant Abraham G. Wolf, whose name was frequently misspelled as "Woolf." According to Colonel Abram Fulkerson, some prisoners believed that Captain Ahl may have been placed at Fort Delaware to spy on General Schoepf and report his conduct to "the authorities at Washington" and that "the harsh prison rules were adopted and enforced by the General at the instance of Captain Ahl." Some prisoners were also of the opinion that Ahl and Wolf deliberately concealed incidences of abuse and corruption from the general, though others were convinced that Schoepf was just as heartless and cruel. One prisoner called Schoepf "a Hessian brute."

No prisoner of war camp was a pleasant place, but Colonel Abram Fulkerson believed Fort Delaware to be "one of the best of Northern prisons" and added that "where large numbers of men, deprived of their liberty, were huddled together…there would be much suffering and complaint."

As in all prison facilities, the rules at Fort Delaware were necessarily strict and strictly enforced. Captain Ahl and Lieutenant Wolf were not only stringent with the Confederate prisoners of war, but they also dealt severely with any offenses committed by the Union soldiers who had been sentenced by army courts-martial to do hard time at Fort Delaware. In his diary, Reverend Handy noted the presence of these "Yankee convicts," some of them restrained by "the ball and chain," and in October 1863, the clergyman described the punishment of two insubordinate Union soldiers by thumb hanging:

> *We had another spectacle of torment this forenoon, in the case of two poor Irishmen…who were hung up by their thumbs and wrists, in front of their own quarters, and in the presence of all their comrades. They were tied by a rope to a cross-beam which was thrown over the parapet,*

This illustration from the Handy diary depicts two insubordinate Union soldiers being hung by their thumbs. The Confederate enlisted men held at Fort Delaware were also subjected to the same treatment. *From the author's collection.*

and then drawn up until they could only just stand upon the ends of their toes. They appeared to suffer very much, and one of them looked every moment as though he would faint from pain and exhaustion. The hands of each were purple and distended with blood. The weaker of the two, finding it impossible to retain his water, was agonized with this additional mortification. This scene of barbarism was under the immediate direction of Capt. Ahl and Provost-Marshall Hawkins; the latter a very pompous and arrogant little fellow, whose disgusting and unfeeling conduct towards prisoners is a subject of constant remark.

The Confederate enlisted men at Fort Delaware were also subjected to this form of torture, and all the prisoners were subject to being "disciplined" by shots fired from their guards. Sometimes these shootings were fatal. In July 1864, Reverend Handy recorded that one of the Confederate officers had been murdered by a guard. The man's name was Colonel Edward Pope Jones, an officer from Virginia. He was lame from a disease that affected his feet and was killed by a sentinel at the prison latrine (which Reverend Handy called a "water-house"). Handy wrote that Colonel Jones "was hobbling along, with one shoe, and was carefully stepping down a rough place, near the water-house, buttoning his pants. He could not have been more than twenty steps from the point of the musket." The guard shot Jones from the roof of the outhouse building, apparently for not moving fast enough. Soon afterward, the other prisoners learned that this soldier was not punished for the shooting but, instead, given a promotion in rank.

Captain Henry C. Dickinson also noted the shooting of Colonel Jones in his diary:

He [Jones] had gotten to some rude steps, some twenty feet to the sink, and was endeavoring to get down; whilst doing so he raised his hand to fix up his suspender, and was in a moment shot down. Lieutenant Brockenbrough, who was under and within four feet of the sentinel, said no warning had been given; others said he called out to him to "double quick" and fired immediately. Rev. Mr. Handy says that the sentinel called to him and that he was ahead of Colonel Jones…At any rate, the fact was undeniable that Jones was orderly, quiet and unobtrusive; that there never had been any orders to us to double quick going to or coming from the sink; that Colonel Jones was very lame—hardly able to walk—and, therefore, could not "double quick," which fact was apparent to the sentinel. Yet he was fired upon, the ball passing through the arm and side. The poor man cried out in his agony, "My God, do not kill me," for lying there he could see the cold-blooded scoundrel reloading his piece.

The prisoners' mail was routinely censored by prison authorities, and apparently no word got to the outside world of this crime, although for three months after the murder, Jones's family members wrote letters to friends in the prison trying to find out any news about him.

The officers who inhabited the wooden barracks outside the fort were somewhat better off than the privates, since they were generally better educated and tended to have more contacts on the outside to whom they could write for help, especially those who came from rich or well-connected families. Captain Henry C. Dickinson recalled, "Many of the officers…had friends in the North, who sent them various articles of food." They could also purchase food and other comforts from the prison sutlers (provisioners who sold goods to the prisoners). The officers who had no money were forced to live off the rations doled out by the authorities, which Dickinson described in the following diary entry:

Our meals were ordered at 8 a.m. and 2 p.m., but were furnished at 10:30 a.m. and 3 p.m. Breakfast consisted of a cup of water, about four ounces of light bread, and say five ounces of pork. Several times the pork was omitted. At dinner we were given a small amount of bread and meat (fresh beef being frequently substituted for salt pork), and in addition, we received a pint of bean soup. This soup was generally burned, and always made of old beans; altogether, it was the most nefarious stuff I ever tasted. We got vinegar twice a week. The fresh beef was fat and could have been made good, but it was killed the day previous and brought into the pen about 9 a.m. covered with a swarm of green flies, and often was so tainted that it could not be eaten…Many men who had no means or friends, finding the meat rations insufficient, caught catfish under the sink (dropping the hook through the holes), and daily lived on this disgustingly filthy food.

Some of the Confederate privates, who also found their rations inadequate, sent complaints about their treatment into the neighboring pen. In May 1864, Reverend Handy described how some of the enlisted men communicated with the officers:

The two pens, occupied severally by officers and privates, are separated by fences, which stand about fifteen or twenty feet apart. These fences are guarded by sentinels who perambulate an elevated platform, from which they may overlook the two enclosures. It requires considerable dexterity to elude the watchfulness of the rough "blue coats" who are there night and day. The cunning "Rebs" have found an expedient in every pebble of suitable weight to secure the necessary impetus for communication across the parapet. Notes are constantly falling into the area on the officers' side, complaining of hard usage by the Yankee authorities, and asking for help or redress from Confederate leaders. Today, one of the little carrier pigeons brought the following to Gen. Vance:

Soldiers' Quarters, Fort Delaware, April 28th, 1864
To Gen. Robert H. Vance, or any other Rebel officer:

Prompted by the gnawing of hunger, I am emboldened to make this appeal to you; hoping that being informed of our sufferings, you can and will appeal to the Commanding General in our behalf, and if possible have our rations increased.

For breakfast we get one-fifth of a loaf of bread, and from four to six ounces of meat—fresh or salt beef, or both—and a pint of very inferior coffee. For dinner we get the same amount of bread and meat—Sunday and Wednesday excepted—when, instead of meat, we get two or three potatoes, and a cup of bean or rice soup. As to supper, we have none.

Whether the rations allowed to us by the authorities and wasted by the cooks, I cannot say, as I do not know. But one thing is certain, we are suffering.

Respectfully, A Hungry Rebel

This note was handed to Gen. Vance, who, feeling it to be his duty to do so, presented it to Gen. Schoepf. The immediate reply was: "Say to them, for their consolation—the rations are to be reduced." The authorities are "shutting down" upon the prisoners, in every part of the island. Officers and privates are, alike, subject to the rigors of this change. Rations are to be reduced.

In his memoir, George H. Moffett, a Confederate private who was brought to Fort Delaware in March 1864, recalled seeing a printed order or bulletin posted in the pen of the enlisted prisoners of war, "emanating from the War Department at Washington":

> *I read it, then reread it again and again until its contents so blistered themselves upon my memory that the scars are still legible. Hence, there can be no mistake in my recollection of it. It began by reciting that it was "a retaliatory measure" in retaliation for hardships imposed upon Union soldiers confined in Rebel prisons, and then proceeded with instructions to commanders of Federal prison posts to reduce the diet of Rebel prisoners under their charge to one-fourth of the regulation allowance for army rations, and to allow no luxuries nor permit surplus comforts. The order was signed "E.M. Stanton, Secretary of War," and was attested by "A. Schoepf, Brigadier General Commanding" and by "G.W. Ahl, Assistant Adjutant General."*
>
> *When I read it, I could scarcely believe my own eyes. Was it possible that there was a civilized government on earth willing to place itself on record in practicing such an enormous barbarity? But there it was in legible characters posted up against the outside wall of the mess hall, near the entrance, in full view of all who cared to stop and read it.*

The retaliatory policy approved by Edwin M. Stanton in 1864 had been justified in part by a pamphlet produced by the Committee on the Conduct of the War, a powerful U.S. congressional committee dominated by the radical faction of the Republican Party. In May 1864, investigating reports of intentional mistreatment of Union prisoners in the South, members of this committee went to a hospital in Annapolis, Maryland, where some ex-prisoners were being treated for illness and wounds. The result of their visit was a thirty-page report (complete with shocking photographs of deathly, emaciated soldiers) that historian William B. Hesseltine described as "a masterpiece of propaganda." The United States government printed and distributed thousands of copies of this official document purporting to offer evidence that the Confederate authorities were maliciously and systematically starving and abusing prisoners of war in their hands. However, some facts were omitted from the committee's report. According to Hesseltine, "No one noticed that two of the pictured men had been dead when the committee visited Annapolis, and no one knew, of course, that the worst case was a soldier who had never been a prisoner at all! Nor did the Committee bother to mention that Confederates had sent these prisoners home, at their own request, because there were no proper hospital facilities for their care in Richmond."

Several months later, the committee's report was followed by a similar publication produced by the United States Sanitary Commission, a relief agency providing medical care for the sick and wounded soldiers of the United States Army. Its 283-page report, entitled *The Narrative of Privations and Sufferings of United States Officers and Soldiers While Prisoners of War*, also included photographs, two of which were borrowed from the earlier congressional document. A "commission of inquiry" appointed by the Sanitary Commission also concluded that there was "a predetermined plan, originating somewhere in the rebel counsels, for destroying and disabling the soldiers of their enemy." The authors of the *Narrative* disputed notions that the Confederate government was unable to provide sufficient rations and supplies for its army and prisoners of war (citing the testimony of some Confederate soldiers) and documented at length and in glowing terms the humane and sanitary conditions in United States prison camps, claiming, among other things, that rations were of good quality and quantity in all Northern facilities and that the shooting of prisoners "was never resorted to unless a rule was grossly and persistently violated."

In response to these two reports, a joint committee of the Confederate Congress presented its own report in early March 1865 concerning the "condition and treatment of prisoners of war." The Confederate legislators emphatically denied Northern accusations of a diabolical "predetermined plan" to destroy helpless prisoners of war and asserted that the "Northern committee" had published the photographs of the sickly prisoners "for the purpose, not of relieving their sufferings, but of bringing a false and slanderous charge against the South."

In its report, the Confederate committee admitted that there was "a vast amount of suffering and fearful mortality among the Federal prisoners at the South," but it placed the blame for these conditions on "the authorities at Washington" and their "settled policy in conducting the war not to exchange prisoners." The Confederate legislators also claimed that their prison system was as humane as possible under the circumstances. Some historians contend otherwise and have written that there was in both prison systems, North and South, a considerable degree of mismanagement, neglect and mistreatment of prisoners. Whatever the case may be, the resumption of exchange, "the obviously humane solution," as William B. Hesseltine put it, would have alleviated much suffering, especially for the men held in the Confederate prison system, overwhelmed as it was, particularly later in the war, with enormous numbers of prisoners to feed and manage. The United States government had it in its power to exchange prisoners yet generally refused to do so in the last half of the conflict, and though other motives for this policy were publicly given out to the people of the North, General Ulysses S. Grant made the carefully calculated decision to put an end to most exchanges as a matter of military strategy: keeping Southern prisoners in captivity helped to deplete the manpower of the Confederate army.

On August 10, 1864, the U.S. secretary of war ordered the elimination of package deliveries to prisoners and also imposed restrictions on trade with the prison sutlers. In his diary, Reveremd Handy noted that these measures caused suffering among the prisoners at Fort Delaware, writing, "Since the embargo on boxes, we have had a constant complaint of hunger. Some men require a great deal more food than others, and these are suffering more or less, all the time, as the Yankee allowance is barely enough, even for those whose appetites are not so keen."

During the summer of 1864, Captain Thomas Pinckney, a prisoner from South Carolina, feared that he would die soon "from a chronic disease caused by bad food and bad water." With such conditions prevailing at Fort Delaware at this time, it is no surprise that reports circulating about an exchange were the cause of jubilation among the Confederate officers. Reverend Handy was in his thirteenth month of confinement at Fort Delaware when he recorded the first intimations that six hundred prisoners were to be taken to South Carolina for exchange, writing on August 12:

> *Great excitement has prevailed all day in consequence of a rumor that six hundred officers are to embark tomorrow, for Hilton Head, South Carolina. Gen. Schoepf came into "the pen" early this morning, attended by several assistants, and remained during the calling of the roll. This is the first time he has ever been present (since I have been in the barracks) on such an occasion. Before he went out, he informed two officers that they would be exchanged in a day or two, with many others…What hope! What buoyancy! How anxious are the thousands here imprisoned, to get back once more to friends and home!*

According to Handy, the selection of the six hundred Confederate officers who were to be taken out of Fort Delaware began the next day.

A day of great excitement. At an early hour the Sergeant came in, and announced that the names of such persons as were to be sent off would soon be called in the yard. All hands were up in a trice; and soon Gen. Schoepf, Capt. Ahl, and sundry clerks, with sergeants and guards, made their appearance. Orders were given to stand on the left of the long walk running through the middle of the open area. Calls were made first for field officers; and then for captains and lieutenants, running down the rolls in an irregular manner, into the M's, and taking a few scattering names farther on in the alphabet. Upon what principle the elections were made, it is impossible to tell. Many were glad; many were disappointed. One man said it made him think of the Day of Judgment. It was certainly very solemn, to see the crowds separating, some to the right, and others remaining on the left. Circumstances indicated the deep feeling, either of joy or regret, experienced by the mass.

It is the prevailing opinion that this movement is the inauguration of a general exchange, and the general feeling is that of buoyancy.

In his diary that day, Lieutenant William E. Johnson, a prisoner from South Carolina, thanked God that he had been chosen as one of the six hundred. John Ogden Murray described what it was like for the prisoners while the roll was being called:

We soon fell into line, the roll call began and went on, while the prisoners stood in death-like silence awaiting the call of their names, each man showing on his face the hope of his heart; each asking God, in silent, earnest prayer, that his name would be called. I have looked into the faces of men in line before a battle, when defeat seemed inevitable; I have seen the joy of victory take the place of doubt; but never in all my life did I witness joy so perfect as in the face of the man whose name was called, nor woe so abject as on the face of the men whose names were passed over. My agitation and suspense was just as great as that of my comrades, and I did silently, away down in the depths of my heart, beg God for deliverance from Fort Delaware. When the M's were called on the roll I could hardly contain myself; when my name was called I could have shouted for joy; and I really felt sorry that not all my comrades were included in the list, as we thought, for exchange. And yet the sequel proved that those whose names were upon the list were the unfortunates, and not those whose names had been passed over. Not dreaming of the terrible fate in store for us and the terrible ordeal we

Confederate prisoners of war waiting to board a steamship at the Fort Delaware wharf. Reverend Handy noted that "about seven hundred and sixty men" departed for exchange in late September 1863. Less than a year later, this scene would be repeated with the departure of the "Immortal Six Hundred." *From the author's collection.*

would be subjected to, we laid down that night upon our hard board bunks and dreamed sweet dreams of home and the welcome awaiting us from loved ones and comrades in Dixie.

The chosen six hundred officers hoped that their departure would be immediate, but they were disappointed and puzzled when several days passed and found them still at Fort Delaware. Reverend Handy noted on August 15, "The suspense of these two days has been almost insupportable. Everything has been in readiness for the removal of the 600 prisoners—the names having been twice called, and the rolls fully arranged but no order comes for the start. All sorts of rumors prevail as to the probable cause of the detention; but all is conjecture, and we remain in the dark."

Finally, on August 20, Reverend Handy wrote, "It was reported that 'the Six Hundred' would certainly leave today."

All were on the qui vive. Presently a sergeant announced, that at 12 o'clock the move would be made…The roll was called, and every man took his place in the ranks, according to the number assigned him about a week ago…After long delay—all being ready—the guards took their places, and the command was given to march through the sally-port to the west end of the "bull-pen." Before this, there had been numberless hand-shakings, and many sorrowful adieus. All were delighted with the prospect of "home again" but there was not a heart there that did not swell with emotion, in the prospect of immediate, and perhaps final separation, from friends and fellow-sufferers in that damp and murky "pen."

As the noble fellows marched out, I stood at the opening of the sally-port, as near as the guards would allow, and until the very last man disappeared from the enclosure, "Good-bye! Good-bye!" was uttered, time and again, as the files moved on, and I could do nothing but return farewells, as some one or more in every rank would wave the parting salutation.

Many good friends left today. A number of them were zealous Christians; several of them young converts; most of them respecters of religion; and a majority, I think, men of unusually good morals. I felt sad, and more than once were my eyes in danger of betraying the deep welling within. Prayers went up to Heaven for the safety and happiness of the brave fellows.

Though hopeful for their good fortune, the clergyman had no way of knowing that these men were exchanging a bad situation for one much worse, and likewise, few of the Confederate officers leaving Fort Delaware that day suspected that they were embarking on a journey into horrendous hardship and suffering.

CHAPTER 2

Under Fire on Morris Island

As Reverend Handy watched six hundred Confederate prisoners of war leaving Fort Delaware on August 20, 1864, he prayed for their safety and happiness, adding, "We shall hope to hear soon of their arrival among friends at the South." Unfortunately, few of these men would enjoy such good fortune. As it happened, most of the six hundred would not be released but would remain in the hands of the enemy under very difficult and extraordinary circumstances. To explain why this group of men was singled out for such treatment, it is helpful to understand the series of events and circumstances leading up to their fateful journey to South Carolina.

Since 1861, the port city of Charleston had been blockaded and besieged by the Federal navy and army, and in the third year of the war, the siege intensified when General Quincy A. Gillmore took command of the Federal forces in that area. In his book *The Siege of Charleston*, Samuel Jones, one of the Confederate generals in command at Charleston, wrote of this time:

> *Charleston was General Gillmore's objective point, which he proposed to gain by way of Morris Island…For the complete success of his plan it was exceedingly important that he should, with the least possible delay, demolish Fort Sumter and silence Fort Moultrie and other batteries on the west of Sullivan's Island, the accomplishment of which formed a part of his plan, and thus open the gate to Charleston for the entrance*

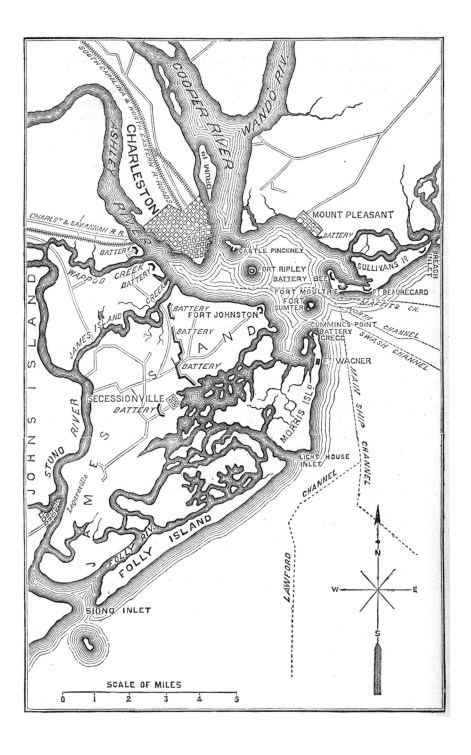

of the fleet before his adversary could prepare other works to bar his approach to the city.

Confederate engineer John Johnson described Gillmore's strategy in the summer of 1863:

The Union commander decided to make [Folly Island] *his base, and concentrated here a force of 10,000 infantry, 350 artillery, and 600 engineer troops, forming a total of nearly eleven thousand men, for a descent from Folly Island upon the southern end of Morris Island, with the design of advancing on Fort Sumter for its reduction, with the closest possible co-operation of the navy.*

Morris Island, located four miles south of Charleston, was a long, narrow, sandy strip of land where the Confederates had placed important defensive fortifications. In July 1863, one of these fortifications, Battery Wagner, was the scene of two assaults by Gillmore's forces. The first attempt to capture Battery Wagner took place on July 10 and 11, 1863. Covered by gunfire from Federal ironclad warships, Union infantry landed on the southern tip of Morris Island, but their attack was repulsed. A little over a week later, there was another unsuccessful assault in which the black soldiers of the Fifty-fourth Massachusetts Regiment famously participated, suffering heavy losses.

Chronicling the second disastrous attack on Battery Wagner, General Samuel Jones listed the various units of the Federal army that took part in this battle, including the Fifty-fourth Massachusetts, and then went on to describe the events of the evening of July 18, 1863:

The First Brigade was formed in column by regiments, except the Fifty-fourth Massachusetts, which…was in column by battalion. It was a negro regiment, recruited in Massachusetts, and was regarded as an admirable and reliable body of men. Half the ground to be traversed before reaching Wagner was undulating with sand hills, which afforded some shelter, but not so much as to prevent free and easy movement; the other half smooth and unobstructed up to the ditch. Within easy range of

Opposite: Map showing the Confederate defensive fortifications in Charleston Harbor. *From the collections of the South Carolina Historical Society.*

Wagner the marsh encroached so much on the firm sand of the island as to leave but a narrow way between it and the water. A few stirring words were addressed by the officers and the men responded with cheers.

About half-past seven the assaulting column was hurled against Wagner, with orders to use their bayonet only, the Federal artillery continuing to fire over their heads as long as it could be done without risk to their own men. The Confederates at their posts were straining their eyes to catch through the deepening twilight the first glimpse of the enemy. When the head of the column came in view a rapid fire of grape and canister was opened, and the fire from James' Island batteries was poured in on the flank. Sumter and Gregg, firing over Wagner, plunged their shot into the advancing column and the parapets of Wagner were lit up by a line of infantry fire…

The advancing column pressed defiantly forward, breasting the storm of iron and lead which was rapidly thinning their ranks…General Strong had urged his command on with great spirit and gallantry, but his losses had been so severe that his regiments were much shaken…Fragments of each regiment, however, brave men bravely led, went eagerly over the ditch, mounted the parapet, and struggled with the foe inside. But their efforts were too feeble to affect the contest materially.

The storm of fire from Wagner had strewn the ditch and glacis with killed and wounded. A few of the bravest of the different regiments, notably the Forty-eighth New York and Sixth Connecticut, continued to press forward…but the brigade had been hopelessly repulsed, its gallant commander, General Strong, was mortally wounded, as was Colonel Chatfield. Colonel Shaw, of the Fifty-fourth Massachusetts, was killed, and many other officers killed and wounded.

The light of the next morning disclosed a ghastly scene of slaughter. The ditch and ground in front of Wagner were thickly strewn with killed and wounded.

At this time in 1863, the Union was already in possession of part of Morris Island and some adjacent marshlands, where it placed its own fortifications and siege guns. According to General Jones, "While approaching Wagner and preparing to demolish Sumter, General Gillmore had made other preparations…He had with difficulty and at much cost constructed a battery known as the 'Swamp Angel,' in the marsh between Morris Island and the Confederate works on James Island, from which Charleston could be bombarded."

General Quincy A. Gillmore (1825–1888). A native of Ohio, he was appointed commander of the Union Southern Department on June 3, 1863. *Library of Congress.*

A Currier & Ives lithograph depicts the ironclad bombardment of Fort Sumter in April 1863. This attack was unsuccessful, but heavy bombardments later that year effectively silenced Fort Sumter's guns. *Library of Congress.*

This photograph of a Union artillery unit was taken during the siege operations against Battery Wagner and Battery Gregg in the summer of 1863. *Library of Congress.*

Despite his failure to take Battery Wagner, General Gillmore continued in his efforts to neutralize Fort Sumter, and in August and September 1863, for sixteen days, the harbor fortress was subjected to heavy bombardments by Union batteries on Morris Island and a squadron of ironclad warships. By September 2, Fort Sumter was demolished, its guns silenced. "The fort had now lost all offensive character," wrote John Johnson, "but it had been firmly decided by the [Confederate] general commanding to hold it in a defensive way to the last extremity."

During this period, the Union batteries on Morris Island also began sending their deadly fire into Charleston, the first attack on the city beginning in the latter part of August 1863. On August 21, 1863, General Gillmore sent a letter to General P.G.T. Beauregard, the Confederate commander in Charleston at that time, demanding the "immediate evacuation of Morris Island and Fort Sumter." If this demand was refused, Gillmore stated that he would "open fire on city of Charleston from batteries already established within easy and effective range of the heart of the city."

Misspelling Gillmore's name, Fitzgerald Ross, a foreign newspaper correspondent in Charleston at the time, wrote about the ultimatum sent to General Beauregard and the initial shelling of the city that began in the middle of the night:

> *Next morning we heard of the "fair warning" General Gilmore had given of his intention to shell the city. It seems that at nine o'clock in the evening a note had been sent to the commanding officer at Fort Wagner to forward to General Beauregard, in which it was demanded that Fort Wagner, Fort Sumter, and the other defences of the harbour, should be immediately given up to the Yankees; if not, the city would be shelled. Four hours were graciously given to General Beauregard to make up his mind, and to remove women and children to a place of safety. The note was entirely anonymous, no one having taken the trouble to sign it. It reached General Beauregard about midnight, and was of course returned for signature and without an answer. At half past-one the shelling commenced. No doubt General Gilmore wished that the effects of the bombardment should have their influence on General Beauregard before it was possible that he should give an answer to the summons…It is rather an extraordinary proceeding, to say the least of it, to bombard the city because the harbour defences, which are three and four miles distant, cannot be taken; and the attempt to destroy it by Greek fire is very abominable; but the spite of the Yankees*

*against Charleston, "the hotbed of the rebellion," is so intense that they
would do anything to gratify it.*

On August 22, 1863, General Beauregard penned an angry reply to
Gillmore's demand for surrender, accusing him of barbarity:

> *Among nations not barbarous the usages of war prescribe that when a
> city is about to be attacked timely notice shall be given by the attacking
> commander, in order that non-combatants may have an opportunity for
> withdrawing beyond its limits. Generally the time allowed is from one
> to three days—that is, time for a withdrawal in good faith of at least
> the women and children. You, Sir, give only four hours, knowing that
> your notice, under existing circumstances, could not reach me in less than
> two hours, and that not less than the same time would be required for an
> answer to be conveyed from this city to Battery Wagner.*
>
> *With this knowledge you threaten to open fire on the city, not to oblige its
> surrender, but to force me to evacuate these works, which you, assisted by a
> great naval force, have been attacking in vain for more than forty days.*
>
> *Batteries Wagner and Gregg are nearly due north from your batteries
> on Morris Island, and in distance therefrom varying from half a mile
> to two and a quarter miles. This city, on the other hand, is to the
> northwest, and quite five miles distant from the battery opened against
> it this morning. It would appear, Sir, that, despairing of reducing these
> works, you now resort to the novel measure of turning your guns against
> the old men, the women and children, and the hospitals of a sleeping
> city—an act of inexcusable barbarity…*
>
> *Your omission to attach your signature to such a grave paper must show
> the recklessness of the course upon which you have adventured, while the
> facts that you knowingly fixed a limit for receiving an answer to your
> demand which it made almost beyond the possibility of receiving any reply
> within that time, and that you actually did open fire and throw a number
> of the most destructive missiles ever used in war into the midst of a city
> taken unawares, and filled with sleeping women and children, will give
> you a bad eminence in history—even in the history of this war.*

Gillmore's reply, also dated August 22, was dismissive of all these
accusations. He blamed the Confederate commander for not having
removed all noncombatants out of Charleston in light of the fact that
that the city was "in the presence of a threatening force" and asserted

that Beauregard could have at least postponed the bombardment of Charleston by agreeing to the demand for the surrender of Fort Sumter and Morris Island. Gillmore concluded, "From various sources, official and otherwise, I am led to believe that most of the women and children of Charleston were long since removed from the city; but, upon your assurance that the city is still 'full' of them, I shall suspend the bombardment until 11 o'clock P.M. tomorrow."

In a letter written to his cousin Mrs. St. Julien Ravenel after the war, Captain Charles C. Pinckney, a Confederate ordnance officer on the staff of General Roswell S. Ripley, recalled the unexpected nighttime shelling of Charleston. Captain Pinckney was roused from his bed that night with orders to report to headquarters:

> *I rode down Smith Street about 2 o'clock A.M. The streets were entirely deserted, yet every house was lighted up. What <u>does</u> it mean? Have the Yankees slipped in and taken the town while I was asleep? I urged the horse, & reached Headquarters. [I asked] "What is it?" "They are shelling the city." "Shelling the city! From where?" "Nobody knows." Shelling the city! Without notice, a city full of sleeping women & children—a bombardment without military significance, and simply an ebullition of spleen at the repeated failure of their attacks…Later on… they shelled the city spasmodically for an indefinite time. We used to sit on the battery at night and see the burning fuses coming across the harbor. I remember that one old negro woman selling groundnuts in the market, was knocked to pieces…The bombardment was absolutely without effect on the progress of the siege, and was clearly & purely spite!*

From August 22 onward until mid-November 1863, only a few more shots were fired into Charleston. After that, the bombardment continued in varying degrees of intensity until February 1865. It lasted 545 days, becoming the longest siege in the history of modern warfare up to that time.

In September 1863, General Beauregard made a decision to evacuate his troops from Morris Island, and Union forces then took possession of the island and all its fortifications. It was at this time, noted John Johnson, that Battery Wagner "came to be called by the Federals a 'fort' after its reputation had been made by stubborn resistance."

In 1864, General John G. Foster took over the command of the Federal forces in South Carolina, and on the other side, General

General Samuel Jones (1819–1887) was a native of Virginia and a graduate of West Point. He was promoted to the rank of brigadier general in the Confederate States Army in April 1862. *Library of Congress.*

Beauregard was replaced by a new commander, General Samuel Jones, who quickly grew frustrated with the relentless bombardment of non-military targets in Charleston. In one of his letters to General Jones, Foster asserted that the whole city of Charleston was a target, since it contained an arsenal and military foundries, but in June 1864, Jones replied to Foster complaining that the bombardment was not accomplishing any military purpose, arguing:

> *The manner in which the fire has been directed from the commencement shows beyond doubt that its object was the destruction of the city itself… and not…to destroy certain military and naval works in and immediately around it; for if* [these] *works…had been the marks, the fire has been so singularly wild and inaccurate that no one who has ever witnessed it would suspect its object…The shells have been thrown at random, at any and all hours, day and night, falling promiscuously in the heart of the city, at points remote from each other and from the* [military and naval] *works…They have not fallen in or been concentrated for any time upon any particular locality, as would have been the case if directed on a particular fixed object for night firing; but they have searched the city in every direction, indicating no purpose or expectation on the part of those directing the fire of accomplishing any military result, but rather the design of destroying private property and killing some persons…most probably women and children quietly sleeping in their accustomed beds… We direct our fire only on your batteries, shipping and troops.*

Hoping to deter the continued shelling of residential and business areas of Charleston, General Jones decided to quarter fifty captive Union officers downtown in a house on the west end of Broad Street owned by Michael P. O'Connor, a prominent Charleston attorney. This house had survived the great Charleston fire of December 1861, though many other buildings surrounding it had been destroyed. In 1863, when the bombardment of the city began, the O'Connor family faced another danger, and as M.P. O'Connor's daughter Mary recorded, like many other Charlestonians, they left the city to seek a safer place to live: "In 1863, residence in Charleston had become dangerous, as the enemy's shells had fallen in many directions, imperiling lives and the safety of homes. A large portion of the population abandoned the city, and a shell having fallen in the vicinity of our home, we left for Columbia, the Capital of the State."

Because few shells subsequently fell in this particular area of Charleston, the placement of the fifty prisoners there amounted to little more than a bluff. When General Foster was informed of their presence in the city, he did not curtail his bombardment but instead requested that an equal number of Confederate officers be placed in a prison on Morris Island in Charleston Harbor, where they would be exposed to the fire of the Confederate batteries and forts.

In a letter of July 1864, Frederick A. Porcher, a prominent Charlestonian, observed that the prisoners on Broad Street were in no danger. Resentful of reports that Confederate prisoners of war were to be placed under fire by the enemy, Porcher expressed his view that the Confederate government should send these captives into a part of the city where they would actually be exposed to fire, "not as they now do, keep them at the extreme West end, where they are perfectly safe."

Five of the prisoners housed on Broad Street were generals in rank, and when they heard of Foster's intentions, they sent him a letter informing him that they were being treated well and requested that the Confederate officers he had sent for also be treated humanely. Their letter, dated July 1, 1864, assured Foster that they were "as pleasantly and comfortably situated as is possible for prisoners of war, receiving from the Confederate authorities every privilege that we could desire or expect, nor are we unnecessarily exposed to fire." The generals who signed the letter were Henry Walton Wessels, Truman Seymour, Eliakim Parker Scammon, Charles Adam Heckman and Alexander Shaler.

On June 27, 1864, Augustine T. Smythe, a young Confederate soldier stationed in Charleston, wrote to his mother about the Federal prisoners quartered at the O'Connor house:

> The Yankees are shelling as usual but nearly all their shells have fallen short. Yesterday, only two or three came in & they burst on the Bay. There was also considerable firing at Sumter, & by our batteries on Gregg, one shot carrying away the flag staff...The Yankee prisoners are in Mr. Conner's house at the corner of Broad & Rutledge Sts. It is a splendid house & a delightful situation. They have a large yard & empty lot to walk in & the other day the Govt. sent round & had gas fixtures put up so that they might have light all at the expense of the Confederacy. They are on their parole not to leave the premises but there is also a guard stationed round them. Great many people go round to see them. They are quite a good looking set, & very well

The O'Connor house on Broad Street, where fifty high-ranking Union prisoners of war were held. The ruins surrounding the O'Connor house were remnants of buildings destroyed in the great fire that swept through Charleston in December 1861. *Library of Congress.*

dressed. Have plenty of money which they spend for coffee & sugar etc. It seems a shame to treat them so well. As we have now got the credit of putting them in shell range, we ought to do so & not leave them out there where a shell does not drop once in two months. They seem perfectly well contented with their situation & well they may be for they are much better off than in camp.

A few days later, on July 1, young Gus Smythe reported in a letter to his sister:

The Yankees have made no reduction of their fire on account of the prisoners in the city, but in retaliation have sent to the North for an equal number of our men, of similar rank, who are to be placed on Morris Island. I doubt if they will be as comfortable as these are. We have them in a fine large house, at the foot of Broad St. with a large open yard for exercise. Yesterday as I passed they were all engaged in a game of cricket & seemed to be enjoying it exceedingly…There is nothing very hard in their lot, as they are now situated.

Captain Henry W. Feilden, an Englishman who was one of General Jones's staff officers, did not approve of Jones's decision to quarter the fifty prisoners in the city. Writing to his fiancée on June 18, 1864, Feilden explained, "Not that I don't consider the brutalities of the Yankees entitle us to exercise the most stringent acts of retaliation. Yet we had kept the escutcheon of our young Confederacy so pure and so unsullied that I had hoped that the future historian would not be able to bring a single act unbecoming a great people against us." In the same letter, however, Feilden vowed that if Confederate prisoners were placed in the midst of military targets as had been threatened, he would support harsh measures in return:

I advocate and shall insist as far as my influence can go on a stern system of retaliation if our men are confined in the batteries on Morris Island to be killed by our guns. Let an equal number of Yanks be placed outside the parapets of Sumter, and if they put our men on the Gunboats and attempt to run in with them, as the silly editor of a Columbia paper suggests, gibbets must be erected on the shore and the Federal Genls hung in view of their friends.

Later in June, Captain Feilden, who was compiling a documentary history of the siege of Charleston, paid a visit to the five generals quartered at the O'Connor house and wrote to his fiancée about it. Feilden was particularly impressed by General Seymour, who had been an officer under the command of Major Robert Anderson at Fort Sumter in 1861 and later led troops in the second ill-fated attack on Battery Wagner:

> *I went down and called on the Federal Genls…I met them, Genl Seymour, Genl Schaller, Wessels, Scammond & Hickman. I have rather an objection to Yankees as you know, but truth obliges me to admit that Seymour is a very pleasant gentleman, well educated, well informed and smart as a steel trap (excuse this vulgarism but it is expressive). I had an hour's pleasant conversation with him. He told me several things which elucidated the report I am now writing of the siege of Charleston, and gave me information I wanted with great frankness, took out his pencil and paper and made me drawings of positions of projectiles and portions of guns. Told me the effective force of the enemy under his command on different occasions &c. I hardly ever met a Yankee before, never a Yankee general and thought that the contact would make one's flesh crawl but strange to say I could not blow Seymour from a gun or hang him without a good deal of repugnance. Indeed I felt more inclined to ask him to dinner and show him around Charleston.*

In response to General Foster's request, fifty Confederate officers were sent down to South Carolina from Fort Delaware, but fortunately for these men and their Union counterparts in the O'Connor house, an agreement of exchange was reached by the two governments, and both groups of prisoners were freed within a matter of weeks.

Later in the summer of 1864, beginning in early August, Union prisoners were being removed from the overcrowded prison camp at Andersonville, Georgia, and General Jones was forced to temporarily accept and incarcerate a large number of captive U.S. officers at several locations in Charleston, including Roper Hospital and the city jail. General Foster's official correspondence of this time indicates that he became aware that these prisoners had not been brought to Charleston to be placed under fire. In a letter to General H.W. Halleck dated August 4, Foster wrote that he knew the prisoners from Georgia had been transferred to Charleston because it was "the only secure place." Two weeks later, on August 18, Foster informed Halleck: "He [Jones] sent

Above: Roper Hospital, where Union prisoners of war were held. Some Charleston nuns (Sisters of Charity of Our Lady of Mercy) visited the prisoners at Roper and cared for their sick. *From the author's collection.*

Opposite: General John G. Foster (1823–1874). A native of New Hampshire, he was General Gillmore's successor as commander of the Union Department of the South. *Library of Congress.*

The Charleston jail, one of several places of confinement for Union prisoners of war in 1864. Nuns of the Sisters of Charity also ministered to the men held here, bringing gifts and medicines. *From the author's collection.*

an apology to General Wessells for placing the 600 officers under fire in Charleston. He stated that he did not place them there to be under fire, but that they were merely en route. The truth is they are so short of men as guards that they have no place to put their prisoners in except Charleston and Savannah."

In the same letter, Foster also stated there would be no injury to the Union prisoners in Charleston from his guns "for I know their exact position and direct the shells accordingly." Early in September, Foster corresponded directly with General Jones, who restated to him that the six hundred Union prisoners were only in Charleston out of necessity and would be removed when arrangements could be made for their accommodation elsewhere. Nevertheless, determining to retaliate once again, General Foster requested six hundred Confederate officers to be sent down to Charleston Harbor to be placed directly in harm's way on

Morris Island. "As soon as the rebel officers arrive," wrote Foster, "I shall place them immediately on Morris Island between Wagner and Gregg."

When the six hundred prisoners Foster requested were selected at Fort Delaware, some of them were wary about their situation, but most clung to the hope that they would be exchanged. Knowing about the fifty Confederate officers who had been sent down to Charleston and exchanged there, they were eager to share the same fate.

In his reminiscences, Colonel Abram Fulkerson noted that the six hundred men who marched out of Fort Delaware in August 1864, many in expectation of exchange, considered themselves "fortunate," but they would discover almost immediately that this was not the case:

> I was one of the 600 selected, and felt very happy at the thought of an early exchange…Poor deluded fellows, little did they dream of the troubles and hardships in store for them…We were marched to the wharf, where we found the steamer "Crescent City," ready for our reception and entertainment, such as it was. When the head of the column passed the gang-way [sic], to our utter astonishment, the guards directed us to pass down a ladder leading from the hatchway into the hold of the vessel, instead of allowing us to go on deck, as we reasonably expected that they would.

Henry C. Dickinson described their plight on the steamer:

> This boat, on which we were destined to spend nineteen long days of great suffering, was an ocean steamer of about 900 tons, and said to be iron-bound. Between decks four rows of bunks had been constructed, each row containing three tiers, and it was calculated that all of us were to stay between decks except at limited times, when a few were allowed to go on deck and get a little air. Between decks there were ports fore and aft on each side, and little air-holes every ten feet, from stern to stern. The bunks and machinery occupied all the room except two passages of three feet. The distance from each bunk to the one above it was about twenty-seven inches, and the bunk in which I stayed with a friend was about three feet wide. The majority of the bunks were dark as night, and those near the machinery were above fever heat at all times. Of course there was no place to sit down or to stand up, therefore, we laid in our bunks day and night. A few, rendered desperate by the heat, would night and day block up the ports, and thus the little air we might otherwise have had was

excluded. Some, who could get no bunks, slept in piles under the steps of the gangway and between the ports. So soon as we were taken aboard a few men, who were favorites of General Schoepf, were taken to the cabin and there slept in beds and ate with the Yankee officers. The wounded and sick, of whom there were about forty, were allowed to sit and sleep on deck around the forecastle gangway, where they were exposed to the sun and rains during the whole trip.

Our guard on board numbered over two hundred muskets. On the first day all were in command of Colonel McCook, of Ohio, who seemed a rather pleasant man and, I think, tried to render us comfortable as the nature of the case would permit...

The sinks of the boat were all upon the upper deck, and two only were allowed to go up at a time, the consequence being that many suffered in this respect. No matter how hot the day was, or how much the men sweltered down between decks, but fifty were allowed to air at any one time. As a consequence, an anxious crowd was always besieging the stairway and many in the stern could not get above at all. Day by day the men became weaker and weaker, until many could scarcely walk at all when we were disembarked.

Another officer, Captain John J. Dunkle of Virginia, wrote a memoir of his experiences that was published in 1869 under the pseudonym Fritz Fuzzlebug. In it he described the departure and initial journey of the Fort Delaware prisoners:

In the latter part of August 1864, we were paraded in Fort Delaware, and after having packed our baggage—consisting of old clothes, and worn out blankets—and bidding farewell to our friends, we were marched to the wharf.

We took passage in a steam-ship called the "Crescent;" into her small hold or middle deck we were quickly crowded—huddled and jammed together like swine on a hog car. We were too many for the capacity of the boat; yet she was made to contain us without inflating her the least.

Imagine our condition; huddled together as close as we could stand; some having room to lie down, while three-fourths had scarcely space upon which to stand. The heat being up to 95° without steam, and of course increasing greatly when the boiler was heated for sailing, great numbers became sea-sick; and then the "stench," "the filth," dirt, &c., in this crowd, was almost intolerable.

The water given us to drink was of an inferior quality, had a disagreeable smell, and a very sickly taste…It was given to us in small quantities, and very frequently we suffered for it…

Our guard consisted of one hundred Ohio militia, commanded by two Lieutenants…They offered many insults to our honor and cause…

The weather was very warm, clear and bright, and no storm or squall disturbed our course. We rounded Cape Hatteras without any difficulty, and if we had been in a comfortable situation, might have enjoyed the voyage…

About three-fourths of us became very sick after leaving Fort Delaware…

We were escorted to the southern waters by a Federal man-of-war, which usually kept close to us, firing a gun over our bow and causing us to heave to, when we got too far out in advance.

Captain George W. Nelson of Virginia recounted his experiences on the voyage:

Bunks had been fixed up for us. They were arranged in three tiers along the whole length of the ship, two rows of three tiers each on each side of the vessel, leaving a very narrow passageway, so narrow that two men could with difficulty squeeze by each other. In the centre of the rows the lower and centre tiers of bunks were shrouded in continual night, the little light through the port holes being cut off by the upper tier of bunks. My bunk, which was about five feet ten inches square, and occupied by four persons, was right against the boiler, occasioning an additional amount of heat, which made the sensation of suffocation almost unbearable. Here we lay in these bunks, packed away like sardines…In two instances the guard placed in with us fainted. I heard one of them remark, "A dog couldn't stand this." Perspiration rolled off us in streams all the time. Clothes and blankets were saturated with it, and constantly dripped from the upper to the lower bunks. Our sufferings were aggravated by a scarcity of water. The water was furnished us was condensed, and so intense was the thirst for it, that it was taken from the condenser almost boiling hot and drunk in that state.

On August 24, the steamer *Crescent City* arrived at Port Royal Harbor, South Carolina. This coastal area of South Carolina south of Charleston, including Hilton Head Island and the town of Beaufort, had been captured and occupied by Federal forces early in the war, Hilton Head becoming the Union army's southern headquarters.

While the ship lay at anchor at Port Royal for several days, the prisoners on board were kept below deck in their miserable, sweltering hold. Captain Dunkle narrated their tribulations:

> At this season of the year the climate in the South is excessively hot, so hot, it can scarcely be borne by Northern or Western persons under ordinary circumstances; much less in our condition—the thermometer being about 96 to 99 degrees.
>
> Added to this immense heat and absence of fresh air, was the heat from the boiler.

Once or twice the prisoners below deck were brought water from the island, but for some reason, this supply soon ceased, and for forty hours they suffered for water in terrific heat. Dunkle continued, "After this horrible agony of forty hours, we were gratified with the return of water. The condensing vessels were put to work, and we were supplied with boiling water…During the remainder of our stay in the boat we had no other for use but boiling water as it ran from the condenser."

Captain George W. Nelson was surprised that no deaths occurred among the prisoners during their journey: "It was strange that none of us died during this trip. I can account for it only by the fact that we were sustained by the hope every one had of being soon exchanged and returning home. Our skins, which were much tanned when we started, were bleached as white as possible during this trip."

Eventually, forty prisoners disabled by wounds or illness were taken off the steamer and sent to nearby Beaufort, and soon afterward, on August 29, the *Crescent City* journeyed on to Charleston, arriving at the harbor there on the first of September. The steamer remained at anchor in the harbor for a number of days, and Henry C. Dickinson wrote of this time:

> We were now fairly under fire, I suppose, and here we remained until the seventh of September, listless spectators of the idleness of the vessels around us, almost dead with heat and hunger and thirst, panting for air and liberty, denied every comfort on earth. Day after day we lingered, in hope that each succeeding day would bring us exchange, or even removal to Morris Island, for even the latter, under

Nathan S. Moseley was a lieutenant in Company F of the Twelfth North Carolina Infantry Regiment. This photograph was almost certainly taken during his imprisonment in Washington or Fort Delaware in 1864. The civilian clothing may have been sent to him or provided from a photographer's stock wardrobe. *From the collections of the South Carolina Historical Society.*

fire of our own forts, was preferable to the insufferable stench of the "Crescent," added to hot water, a bare modicum of crackers and salt pork, and the daily danger of the equinoctial storm, which might drive us to sea without water or food. Many of the men, I am certain, were almost crazed by the mental and bodily torture they suffered during these long days and nights.

On September 7, the Confederate prisoners disembarked at Morris Island. Not long after his arrival on the island, Lieutenant Nathan S. Moseley, a prisoner from North Carolina, wrote a letter to an acquaintance in the city of Charleston, Mr. William C. Bee. Moseley had been wounded and captured at Spotsylvania Court House in Virginia on May 12, 1864, and spent about six weeks at the Lincoln General Hospital in Washington, D.C., before being transferred to the Old

Capitol Prison and then to Fort Delaware. While in the hospital he had taken care of Mr. Bee's son James, a wounded fellow prisoner. Shortly after the amputation of a leg, James Bee died, and Lieutenant Moseley penned a touching letter to his father informing him of the sad news. At Morris Island, Moseley renewed his correspondence with Mr. William C. Bee, possibly hoping to receive some help from him. Knowing that his letter would be examined by prison authorities, Moseley struck a hopeful tone and offered few complaints about the voyage on the steamer *Crescent City*, writing on September 8, 1864:

> *We landed here yesterday after 18 days very uncomfortably on board the Steamer Crescent. We left Ft. Delaware 20 Augt. Our voyage was pleasant with the exception of the crowd of our men on board. Suffered very much from the effects of heat. I feel better satisfied, although we are placed under different circumstances. I hope it will not be long before we shall be liberated, and enjoy the pleasures we once so much delighted in. I hope to hear from you soon.*

Captain Henry C. Dickinson's diary gave this account of the arrival of the Confederate officers at Morris Island:

> *We were met at the wharf by a full regiment of the Sons of Africa, the Fifty-fourth Massachusetts, under command of Colonel Hallowell, son of an abolition silk merchant in Philadelphia. This regiment (whilst the Yanks were getting us off and taking away our blanket, which latter, by the way, they only partially replaced) amused us by exhibiting their proficiency in the manual [i.e., rifle drill], and thus, as they supposed, impressing us with a wholesome dread of their prowess. We soon started up the eastern beach of Morris Island, guarded as closely by these negroes as if we were in Confederate lines. The gait was so rapid and we so weak that many of us utterly broke down about one and one-half miles from the wharf, when we halted to rest, and, as it just commenced raining hard, we eagerly caught water in our hats to drink, having had none for twenty-four hours. The negroes, perceiving this, went to a spring hard by and brought us some very good water.*

Another prisoner, Lieutenant Henry Howe Cook from Tennessee, recorded the following impressions of his arrival and first days on Morris Island:

The prison stockade on Morris Island, 1864, as seen from the interior. *Library of Congress.*

On reaching shore we were placed under the charge of the Fifty-fourth Massachusetts Regiment. I do not know why it was called the Fifty-fourth Massachusetts, as its colonel, Hallowell, was from Philadelphia, while its privates and non-commissioned officers were negroes from the Southern states, though some of the commissioned officers were from Massachusetts. I often talked with a young lieutenant of this regiment, who thought that the war was being fought solely to free the negroes. He was of the class who thought that the Constitution was a league with the powers of evil. In charge of this regiment, we marched into our prison pen, situated midway between Forts Wagner and Gregg. Our prison home was a stockade made of palmetto logs driven into the sand, and was about one hundred and thirty yards square. In this were small tents and ten feet from the wall of the pen was stretched a rope, known as the "dead-line." Outside of the pen, and near the top of the wall, was a walk for the sentinels, so situated as to enable them to overlook the prisoners. About three miles distant, and in full view, was Charleston, into which the enemy was pouring heavy shells during the night while we remained on the island. [Fort] Sumter lay a shapeless mass about twelve hundred yards to the west of us, and from it our sharpshooters kept up a constant fire upon the artillerymen in Fort Gregg. Off to the right lay Sullivan's Island, and we could see the Confederate flag floating over [Fort] Moultrie.

The first evening remained quiet, not a shot being fired by Moultrie or Wagner. Late in the evening I watched the great bombshells sent from Gregg into the city of Charleston, and heard one loud report from the "Swamp Angel," situated about six hundred yards southeast of us. At sunset we were ordered into our tents, there to remain until sunrise the next day. In the morning we received our first meal upon the island. This consisted of two moldy crackers and two ounces of boiled pickled meat, while at four o'clock in the afternoon we were given two crackers and a gill [one-quarter pint] of bean soup. Two negro soldiers carried the rations around to the tents…

In the evening of the second day Wagner opened fire on Moultrie. Soon Gregg opened fire, and the two made the sand island quiver and shake as if it would melt from under us. For several hours this continued, Moultrie remaining silent. Our friends knew that we were staked between Wagner and Gregg. A little after dark a boom from that direction gave notice that old Moultrie would remain silent no longer. I watched the fiery globe as it curved gracefully in the air and descended with frightful rapidity right

Forts Wagner and Gregg on Morris Island. *Library of Congress.*

upon me, as it seemed, but it passed over into the garrison of Wagner. I sat in the door of my tent and watched the battle. The whole heavens were illuminated and the mortar-shells were darting through the heavens in all directions as though the sky were full of meteors…The firing continued at night during the entire six weeks of our stay on the island, but I think that the battle of the second night was much the fiercest of any of these artillery duels.

From a "lofty perch behind a big telescope," as he put it, Gus Smythe observed the actions of the enemy in Charleston. Assigned to the signal corps, Gus was stationed high above the city in the steeple of St. Michael's Church, and from there he could look out on the harbor and all its surrounding forts and batteries. On September 8, 1864, he wrote to a cousin:

Well I think the Yankees have got our men on Morris Island at last. They have them in a large pen, a piece of ground surrounded by a high fence, with no shelter, merely the bare sand enclosed by this barricade. It is closely watched by sentinels who are stationed all around it, mounted upon the outside so as to be able to over look the fence, & the whole place inside. This pen has been completed for some little time, but the prisoners were only introduced yesterday & today they seem to have put in quite a number. This is not positive yet, for we have no certain, no official notification of the fact, but it is extremely probable & tallies with the expressed intentions…of the Yankees. Oh! wont it be cold during the piercing winds of this winter on that bleak beach with no shelter! I think they may have as an object, the forcing us to an exchange of officers alone & I trust if they do propose anything of the kind, we shall be firm enough to refuse it. It would be base to desert the poor privates in prison.

On that same day, Gus wrote to his mother:

No news save the belief & very probable almost certain, that the Yankees have put our prisoners in their hands, on Morris Isl. at last. They erected some time ago in the sand between Wagner & Gregg, a large stockade or fence, about 8 or 10 ft. high enclosing a portion of the Island. We at first supposed it a breakwater to keep out the tides, but two or three days ago a large transport with men on board, crowded, came in from Hilton

Head & yesterday & all to-day they have been introducing men into this pen, which is also strongly guarded by sentinels, who march around on platforms or shelves, fastened to the fence, about 4 ft. from the ground so that each sentinel can over see the whole pen at a glance. I can see no sign of shelter, except what looks as tho' it might be a couple of small tents, but I do not think so, & I can see the men in the morning getting their rations & also see the poor fellows looking through the cracks of the fence. How tantalizing to them & us, thus to be within sight of each other, but so out of reach!

While Gus Smythe watched from his steeple post, the prisoners on Morris Island, especially those from South Carolina, must have been wondering how much damage the continual enemy bombardment was doing in the city. On September 28, Gus penned another letter to his mother about the shells being thrown into Charleston:

While keeping my watch up here, I shall employ my time in writing to you…The Yankees are throwing in their shells at a tremendous rate, one every two or three minutes since 5 o'clock, now it is 10 P.M. & before that all morning at the rate of one every 5 minutes. Since 8 A.M. they have thrown 114 shells up to 9:45 P.M. Now they have stopped but there is no saying for how long the cessation will continue. And the shells too are not dropping down town, & very few in the water, but up they go to Chapel & Ann Sts. & all around there. One an hour or so ago went into Mr. Carr's house in Aiken's Row. The family had just left the parlor & seated themselves at the supper table when the shell went into the room they had left & burst, knocking the chairs about & making havoc all around. One two or three days ago went into Wolfe St.! Citadel Green is a command resort. The Citadel Square Church was hit the other day, & very much damaged & the same with Grace Church…Surely they have done enough for to-day. They are now using some three or four guns, one of them a 200 pdr. & they do have an enormous range. The report comes to us that they are manufacturing them to shoot still farther, so as to command the entire city. Won't we have a jolly time then! As far as we are personally concerned, it is a benefit, for now we are only troubled with a time fuze shell every now & then, by far the greater majority go up town…The damage done to the City is beginning to mount up & if they keep on at this rate will be very great. But how much better off are we than the poor citizens of Atlanta, Memphis & so many other of our cities. If they let us off with the shelling we should be thankful. I used to feel very much like grumbling up here, but since they have put our poor fellows in that Pen on Morris Isl. whenever I begin to complain & happen to cast my eye over there it hushes me up at once. Oh Mother! amidst all our troubles & privations how much have we to be grateful for: that we are still an united unbroken family, not one member even maimed, our home, tho' in the reach of Yankee missiles, still out of their hands & so little injured, & you all, tho' not so well placed as you were here, still with a comfortable shelter, where you can at least obtain the necessaries of life & feel secure, as secure as possible, from the invasion of our vandal foes...

Have been down stairs to get the Sergeant of Police to carry a letter up for me to the Office which Locke, my chum, forgot to mail this afternoon. He tells me that a shell went into Mr. Burckmyer's house in Charlotte St. this afternoon & wounded more or less severely all his family, five in number...Also that again to-day the Citadel Square Church was hit, & Zion very much damaged by one, & St. Joseph's, the old Anson St. church, also struck...So the cry is still they come. And as an incentive to matrimonial harmony...a man named Burgess had fallen out with his wife, & two evenings ago they were cooking supper, one upstairs & the other in the room below, when a shell came in where he was, struck the fire place & a brick hit him on the head injuring him so badly that to-day he died from the effects of it.

At night, the prisoners on Morris Island would watch the spectacle of artillery fire in the skies over the harbor. Captain Henry C. Dickinson chronicled the battles witnessed by the prisoners there in September and October 1864:

On the evening of the ninth of September at 4 p.m. Battery Wagner commenced firing shotted guns in honor of the Atlanta victory, directing her fire upon Sumpter [sic] and Moultrie. Old Moultrie at last became aroused and returned the compliment, and both parties up this engagement, directly over our heads, till after 10 p.m....

In this engagement Moultrie fired splendidly, only two or three shots falling too short; the great majority fell into Wagner. Most of our shells were from mortars and looked as if they would fall directly on us, but, whilst we held our breath in anxious expectation, its parabolic course

Federal artillery on Morris Island sending shells into the city of Charleston. *From the collections of the South Carolina Historical Society.*

would land it in the fort. Every good shot was applauded by us as loudly as we dared. We were but 250 yards from the spot at which these monster shells were directed, and too little powder or a slight elevation of the mortar might have killed many of us since we were so crowded together. But it was a trial of Southern against Northern gunnery… Two shells exploded over us throwing great and small pieces all about our camp. After these two last shots Moultrie fired no more at Wagner, and this was the first evidence that the Confederates knew our position between the forts…

About the first of October one of the large guns at Gregg exploded, killing two men. Work on so extensive a scale in that neighborhood seemed to betoken more activity in firing on Charleston…Old Sumpter could be seen from our northwest corner, and at daybreak she generally had her sharpshooters busy who made all hands keep their head low. Occasionally the picket monitor opened on Sumpter and Moultrie, and the "Swamp Angel" fired at Charleston, whilst "Bull of the Woods," as the Yanks called it, on James Island, returned the compliment on Gregg.

On the night of the sixth of October, when the firing was excessive at a late hour, two of our shells exploded, throwing large pieces over our camp, though they did not damage us. I daily expected the enemy to make an attack on Charleston...It was said that...all six huge guns at and near Gregg were bearing on Charleston. Almost every day we could see the smoke of a huge fire, the work of these incendiaries who fought a nation by killing women and children and burning houses.

The fortifications on Morris Island occupied by the Federal troops were targeted by the Confederate gunners and sharpshooters from four points—Fort Moultrie on Sullivan's Island, Fort Sumter in the harbor and Fort Johnson and Battery Simkins on James Island—and though the stockade prison was situated between Batteries Wagner and Gregg, the constant targets of artillery fire, none of the prisoners was killed by the shells sent in from the Confederate installations. Like Captain Dickinson, many of the officers believed that the Confederate artillerymen knew their exact position on the island and aimed over them. Colonel Abram Fulkerson noted that "the Confederates fire with such precision that not a single shot or shell fell within our stockade, and but one shell exploded immediately over us." In contrast, General John G. Foster, writing to General H.W. Halleck about the prison stockade on September 19, 1864, reported, "The rebels, in firing on Morris Island, do not endeavor to avoid this camp, and although the shot and shell fall all around no one has yet received any injury." At least one prisoner, Henry E. Handerson, never felt himself in any danger and considered the retaliatory placement of the Confederates on Morris Island a "farce," the only purpose of which was to generate propaganda that would gin up more war fever in the North.

Francis C. Barnes, an officer from Virginia, recalled:

After landing at Morris Island we were placed under the fire of our own guns in front of a Federal battery...The first evening and night the shelling was very heavy but none of us were killed. It seemed our guns got the range and fired over us. One morning while Captain Findley...J.E. Cobb, H. Coffry and myself were in our small tent just after Captain Findley read a chapter in the Bible...a large shell fell right at our feet and covered us all with sand, but fortunately did not explode nor break up our accustomed worship.

We were guarded by negro troops commanded by Colonel Hallowell, who was a heartless man, and under him the most cruel treatment was experienced. We were…often fired into by the guards for the most trivial offence and several men were wounded.

John Ogden Murray gave a similar assessment of the commandant:

Colonel Hallowell, with whom we were brought in more contact than any other officer—for the reason he had full control of our pen—was about the meanest fellow our misfortunes brought us in connection with; in fact, the negroes he commanded were Chesterfields in politeness compared with this fellow. After we had been some weeks in the stockade under the fire of our own guns…this doughty colonel one afternoon came into the stockade, had us drawn up in line, and made the following speech which I have never forgotten. He said: "The fate of war has placed you prisoners in my hands, and I will treat you as prisoners. I feel it my bounded duty to fight men who have raised their unhallowed hands against their country's flag. But I will try and treat you as men, as you have fallen into my hands, and this will be my duty so long as you obey the rules and orders laid down for the government of this prison." But he did not keep his word. He treated us like animals, and he did not intend to treat us like men when he said he would do so. He violated every promise he ever made us, both in the spirit and letter; there was nothing this fellow left undone to make us uncomfortable and annoy us; he never let one opportunity pass to show his hatred for the South and her soldiers. And yet in our six hundred prisoners were the sons and grandsons of ancestors who had helped make American history and consecrate the American flag.

Captain George W. Nelson also described Colonel Hallowell and his treatment of the prisoners and soldiers under his command:

I always felt in his presence as if I had suddenly come upon a snake. He [Hallowell] used frequently to come into the pen and talk with some of the prisoners. He seemed to take a fiendish pleasure in our sufferings. A prisoner said to him on one occasion: "Colonel, unless you give us more to eat, we will starve." His reply was: "If I had my way I would feed you on an oiled rag." Once he told us we must bury the refuse bones in the sand to prevent any bad smell from them. One of our number answered: "If you don't give us something more to eat, there will not only be nothing

The prison stockade on Morris Island, exterior view. *Library of Congress.*

to bury, but there won't be any of us left to bury it." "Ah, well," he replied, "when you commence to stink, I'll put you in the ground, too."

Our camp was laid off in streets, two rows of tents facing each other, making a street…A negro sergeant had charge of each row, calling it "his company." These sergeants were generally kind to us, expressed their sorrow that we had so little to eat. We had a point in common with them, viz: intense hatred of their Colonel. Their hatred of him was equaled only by their fear of him. His treatment of them, for the least violation of orders, was barbarous. He would ride at them, knock and beat them over the head with his sabre, or draw his pistol and shoot at them.

An order issued on September 7, 1864, laid out the rules for the government of the prison camp on Morris Island. According to these regulations, the prisoners were divided into eight detachments of seventy-five men, and each unit of seventy-five was under the charge of a warden. There were three roll calls every day—the first at dawn, the second at noon and the third an hour before sunset. No prisoners were allowed to leave their tents after nightfall, and their movements within camp during the day were limited to the area marked out by the rope deadlines. Prisoners who crossed the deadline "under any pretence" would be shot by sentries. Any disturbances or disorder among the prisoners in the camp would also be dealt with by gunfire. The prisoners could write one half-page letter each week, and all their letters were opened and inspected by the provost marshal before leaving the island. As for their meals, breakfast was at 7:00 a.m., dinner at 12:00 p.m. and supper at 5:00 p.m. Captain George W. Nelson remembered that "a little mush or rice" was issued for supper, but according to John Ogden Murray, the last meal of the day apparently only appeared on paper, at least for some length of time. "Our rations, under this order," he wrote, "was a menu for wooden gods."

It consisted of four hardtack army crackers, often rotten and green with mold, and one ounce of fat meat, issued to us at morning roll call; for dinner, we received one-half pint of bean or rice soup, made as the caprice of the cook suggested; for supper, we were allowed all the wind we could inhale…Our drinking water was obtained by digging holes in the sand, and then waiting until sufficient very insipid water would ooze out of the sand to quench thirst.

Lieutenant Henry H. Cook noted that "sickness soon began to prevail" among the prisoners on Morris Island, and some began to suffer from dysentery, an inflammation of the bowels that causes severe diarrhea, spasmodic pains and cramps and bloody discharges.

It must have been especially tantalizing for the captive officers from South Carolina to be so close to home. Captain Thomas Pinckney, who bore one of the most honored family names in South Carolina history, was one of these. He was the great-grandson of Eliza Lucas Pinckney, an important agriculturalist, and the grandson of Rebecca Brewton Motte, a heroine of the Revolution. When the war began, Pinckney raised his own company of cavalry and carried into battle with him the sword his grandfather Major General Thomas Pinckney had used in his service during America's fight for independence from the British as well as the War of 1812. The sword was captured, along with the captain, at the Battle of Hawe's Shop in Virginia by Lieutenant James Ingersoll of Custer's Division and was not returned to its owner.

Decades after the war, Captain Pinckney penned his "Reminiscences," and at that time, looking through the United States government's official records of the so-called War of the Rebellion, he found a report stating that the daily rations issued to the prisoners on Morris Island were the following: "three-quarters of a pound of fresh beef, or one-half pound of salt meat, one-half pound of hard bread or one-half pint of meal, one-fifth pint of rice, and the same of beans, with a small allowance of salt and vinegar." Pinckney's comments on this were, "I certainly never received the rations here described, nor do I believe they were ever issued to our prisoners, as many alive can testify."

Captain Henry C. Dickinson also described the inadequate diet of the prisoners:

The provost marshal was, I am told, charged with the duty of feeding us, the negro sergeants furnishing it to us. The meat was taken out of the box with their hands generally full of sand, and the soup was dipped out of a small barrel. On hot days the sweat from the negroes was plentifully mixed with the soup. During the first few days when the scanty ration was issued the negroes were so much ashamed that they apologized by saying it was new to the officer, and he would do better in the future, but it was soon apparent that there was a determination to make us live down to the very lowest limit capable of sustaining life. Until about the first of October we had daily three, sometimes four, and sometimes only two, small crackers per diem, about one-fourth pound of meat, frequently one-eighth, one gill of thin bean soup, and one gill of cooked rice. This was absolutely all we got and consequently we were always hungry. So extreme was the hunger of some that they dug with their hands for grass roots for subsistence. The crackers issued to us were always full of worms and bugs, frequently mere scrapings of a box, and would have been condemned by any medical board as unfit for food.

Henry E. Handerson recalled that the boiled rice the prisoners were served for breakfast was "usually full of worms." In October, Dickinson reported that rations improved:

About the first of October a Yankee colonel, exchanged, came in the pen and commenced telling us what rations he received at Charleston. Colonel Hallowell was with him and exhibited to him the orders requiring that we should be fed as the prisoners in Charleston. The order was not read out and we then found out that someone had been daily cheating us of the rations ordered to us. After this so much complaint was made, and the sick list had increased to such an extent that Doctor Durrant, the surgeon, took the trouble to search into the affair; the result was that following the investigation we received daily about five crackers and one-fourth pound of meat, except one day, when our friends in Charleston sent us something, the Yanks gave us nothing. The Yankees insisted on giving us a gill of soup and cooked rice, although the prisoners in Charleston got daily one-fifth of a pint of raw beans and rice, which, cooked, would make twice the quantity we got.

At this time, some unusual events occurred that gave the Confederate officers cause to believe that they would be exchanged. These hopes were soon dashed, but not long afterward, as John Ogden Murray recorded, they learned that there was at least hope of leaving Morris Island:

We had now been on Morris Island several weeks, suffering the pangs of starvation, and every man bearing himself with dignity and courage through the trying ordeal. One morning in October, to our surprise, the guns of old Sumter, Charleston, Moultrie, and Johnson were silent. We could not divine why, and began to make all kinds of surmises. The negro guards and their officers walked leisurely about, without the fearful look they generally bore. After a long time we ascertained, from one of the negro sergeants in charge of our camp, that the Confederate government had demanded our removal from under fire and off of Morris Island, or they were going to place six hundred officers (Federal prisoners of war) on the ramparts of Fort Sumter. He also stated that General Foster, commanding United States forces, had asked for a flag of truce conference, which was then in session. We could see the men on Fort Sumter's ramparts. All was as serene as a church picnic. Later on, this negro sergeant informed us that the Secretary of War, himself, from Washington, was on the flag of truce boat with his cabinet, and was making arrangements to exchange all the prisoners of war, colored troops included. We were, of course, elated at this information, and speculation, rumors and "grape" filled the camp. At sundown the guns of Charleston, Sumter, and the Yankee guns on Morris Island began booming; then we knew there was to be no exchange; but next morning the guns were again silent, the flag of truce boats were again together. At evening roll call the negro sergeant informed us exchange had been accomplished. To confirm this Colonel Hallowell informed us he was going to be rid of us at last, and ordered us to be ready at daylight the next morning to move out of the stockade and off the island, for exchange. At daylight we were ordered into line; out of the stockade prison we marched, down the beach to the old schooner hulks, which were utilized as our prison when we first landed on the island. We were packed on board of these old schooners, the "Transit" and "J.A. Genet," where we remained thirty-six hours while the flag of truce boats were together off Fort Sumter. The conference failed to agree upon an exchange and we were marched back into the stockade prison pen in the afternoon, to again face the rigors of retaliation and brutality…On our return to the prison pen, from our march down the beach, our hearts were made glad by a lot of boxes and tobacco, sweet potatoes, and peanuts our government had sent us under flag of truce. This renewed our strength, and we were all grateful…

After several days we were again ordered to pack up and be ready to move at daylight from the prison pen…When the order came to move out of the stockade pen we thanked God exchange had come at last. We would soon be free men…But, alas, disappointment awaited us; hope was to be ousted from our hearts by despair, and fate had in store for us a harder ordeal. As we marched down the beach to once more board the schooner hulks our hearts were glad, but before the sun set we knew exchange was not for us. Before leaving Morris Island all blankets marked U.S. were taken from those who had them. This was done by order, we were told, of

General Foster…After a short delay at Morris Island wharf, a gunboat took us in tow for Fort Pulaski.

During their sojourn on Morris Island, three of the Confederate prisoners died of disease and deprivation. One of them was Lieutenant Frank P. Peake of Kentucky, who was stricken with acute dysentery. John Ogden Murray tried to get medical help for the lieutenant when it became apparent in late September that he was seriously ill, but days passed before the prison doctor came to give him any attention, and by the time the physician arrived, the sick man was beyond all help. According to Murray, Lieutenant Peake died on October 2, 1864, and was buried by his comrades. "In the twilight," wrote Murray, "we dug him a grave in the sands of Morris Island, and laid him to rest, while the shot and the shells…sang his funeral dirge."

CHAPTER 3

Prison Life at Fort Pulaski

In the latter part of October 1864, the Confederate prisoners were told that they would be leaving Morris Island. At this time, according to John Ogden Murray, "it was the general impression, as we marched out of the pen, that we were to be exchanged." Thinking that he would soon be a free man, Murray was emboldened to express some choice parting words to Colonel Hallowell:

> [Hallowell] *was standing at the prison gate, glaring at us as we passed out. We were marching by fours; in the fours just ahead of me was Capt. Bruce Gibson, Maj. W.W. Goldsborough, and two other officers whose identity I now forget. When I reached Hallowell I halted and said, "You yellow-faced scoundrel, we are going back home now, and I hope and pray to God that it may be my fortune to get my hands on you, that the world may be rid of such a brute." His face turned livid with rage. He shouted out to one of the guards to shoot that man, meaning me; but the guard pointed his gun direct at Capt. Bruce Gibson, and would have killed him but for the order of one of the negro sergeants to put down his gun. By this time the line had passed Hallowell, and Captain Gibson was saved. I never in all my life was so unstrung; my foolish temper had almost cost an innocent life—the life of my best friend. After this incident my temper was kept under control.*

Lieutenant Henry H. Cook recalled:

> [We] *were informed that we were to be taken to Fort Pulaski, at the mouth of the Savannah River. We were in the hands of Foster, and no mercy was expected or hoped for. We staggered or were hauled to the wharf and were placed upon the little schooners to be towed to Fort Pulaski. The horrors of Morris Island were not to be compared with what awaited us on the coast of Georgia.*

Captain George W. Nelson remembered his ravenous hunger on the day the prisoners were removed from the island:

> *About the 18th of October we were drawn up in a line, three days' rations were issued, viz: fifteen "hard tack" [crackers] and a right good-sized piece of meat. I felt myself a rich man. I remember well the loving looks I cast upon my dear victuals, and the tender care with which I adjusted and carried my trusty old haversack. A few minutes more and we took up the line of march for the lower end of Morris Island, with a heavy line of darkey guards on either side. The distance was only three miles, but this to men confined for over a year, and for two months previous existing upon such light rations, was a very considerable matter. Several of our number gave out completely, and had to be hauled the remaining distance...We were put in two old hulks fitted up for us, and then were towed out to sea. The first evening of the journey I fell upon my "victuals," and was so hungry that I ate my three days' rations at once. To a question from a friend, "What will you do for the rest of the time?" I replied: "I reckon the Lord will provide." But I made a mistake. I might have known the Almighty would use such instruments as were about us as ministers of wrath. The evening of the third day we anchored off Fort Pulaski. By this time I was nearly famished.*

Fort Pulaski had been in Union hands since its capture in 1862. Engineer John Johnson described this Confederate defense facility on the Georgia coast near Savannah as a "casemated brick fort, of the same period as Fort Sumter and very like it, except in having only one tier of casemates; garrisoned with 385 men; armed with five 10-inch and nine 8-inch smoothbore columbiads, three 42-pounders, twenty 24-pounders (Blakely), and five mortars, making a total of 39 guns and 5 mortars."

Fort Pulaski, located on Cockspur Island on the Georgia coast. The fort was captured by Union forces in April 1862. *From the collections of the South Carolina Historical Society.*

Nearby Tybee Island had been abandoned by the Confederate forces in late 1861, and the Union eventually took advantage of this opportunity to move its troops here, erecting eleven batteries along the northwest shore from which to shell Fort Pulaski.

Quincy A. Gillmore, then a captain in the engineers, was in command of the Union forces on Tybee, and in April 1862, after a bombardment of a day and a half from Union batteries, wrote Johnson, "total shots fired 5275, with a breaching cannonade of nine and a half hours, the fort surrendered, its magazine being in immediate danger."

The volume of *Confederate Military History* relating to the war in Georgia gives this account of the battle for Fort Pulaski:

> *Within the walls of Fort Pulaski, under the command of Col. Charles H. Olmstead, were a little over 400 men of the Savannah regiment, or First regiment of Georgia…The fight went against the fort from the first, but there was great faith in the strength of the works. Gen. David Hunter, commanding the Federal department of the South, demanded the surrender of the garrison of Colonel Olmstead, the flag [of truce] being sent under Lieut. James H. Wilson. Colonel Olmstead replied briefly, declining to surrender, and stating that he was there "to defend*

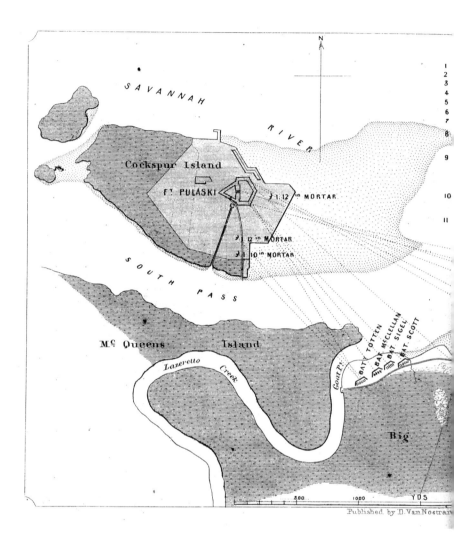

Published by D. Van Nostran

the fort, not to surrender it." The first shell was fired at 8:15 on the morning of April 10, 1862, and by 9:30 all the beleaguering batteries were in operation. Colonel Olmstead replied vigorously, but was at a disadvantage at the start on account of knowing the position of but two of the eleven Federal batteries. An attack by the Federal fleet was anticipated, but it took no part in the bombardment. The Confederate soldiers and citizens in Savannah and the adjacent fortifications listened with anxiety throughout the day to the continuous roar of the guns. The ten hours' bombardment on the first day caused no material damage, but during that night the garrison was terribly harassed by the enemy's

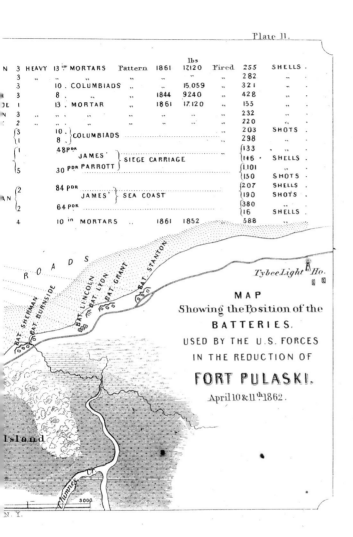

Plate II.

					lbs				
N	3	HEAVY	13 ᵗ MORTARS	Pattern	1861	17.120	Fired	255	SHELLS .
	3	"	" "	"	"	"	"	282	" .
	3		10 . COLUMBIADS	"		15.059	"	321	" .
	3		8 . "	"	1844	9240	"	428	" .
JE	I		13 . MORTAR	"	1861	17.120	"	155	" .
N	3	"	" " "	"	"	"	"	232	" .
	2	"	" " "	"	"	"	"	220	" .
	3		10 . } COLUMBIADS				"	203	SHOTS .
			8 . }					298	" .
	I		48 ᴾᴰᴿ JAMES' } SIEGE CARRIAGE					133	" " .
	5		30 ᴾᴰᴿ PARROTT }					146 ·	SHELLS .
								1.101	" .
								150	SHOTS ·
	2		84 ᴾᴰᴿ JAMES' } SEA COAST					207	SHELLS .
								190	SHOTS .
	2		64 ᴾᴰᴿ					380	" .
								16	SHELLS .
	4		10 ⁱⁿ MORTARS	"	1861	1852		588	" .

TybeeLight Ho.

MAP

Showing the Position of the

BATTERIES.

USED BY THE U.S. FORCES

IN THE REDUCTION OF

FORT PULASKI.

April 10 & 11ᵗʰ 1862 .

Map of the siege of Fort Pulaski, 1862. *From the collections of the South Carolina Historical Society.*

mortar shells which were dropped into the fort, one every five minutes. A fiercer attack began at daybreak of the second day, especially upon the southeast angle, where the fire of the rifled cannon was concentrated to breach the walls of the fort...

The officers' quarters were torn to pieces, the bomb-proof timbers scattered in every direction over the yard, and the gates to the entrance knocked off. The parapet walls on the Tybee [Island] side were all gone, in many places down to the level of the earth on the casemates. The protection to the magazine in the northwest angle of the fort had all been *shot away; the entire corner of the magazine next to the passageway was shot off, and the powder exposed, while three shots had actually penetrated the chamber. Such was the condition of affairs when Colonel Olmstead called a council of officers in a casemate; and without a dissenting voice they acquiesced in the necessity of a capitulation, in order to save the garrison from utter destruction by an explosion, which was momentarily threatened. Accordingly, at 2 o'clock p.m. the men were called from the guns and the flag was lowered...The terms of capitulation provided that the sick and wounded should be sent under a flag of truce to the Confederate lines, but this General Hunter afterward declined to ratify... and the whole garrison was sent as prisoners to the forts in New York harbor. The Federals contented themselves with occupying the fort, thus closing the port* [of Savannah] *to commerce.*

Captain Henry Dickinson noticed the effects of the 1862 siege as their ship approached Fort Pulaski:

At daybreak we are in sight of the Georgia shore, and about sunrise enter Savannah River; passing Tybee Island, we anchor in the southern channel, under the guns of Fort Pulaski.

The southern wall of the fort, about one hundred yards long and arranged for one tier and parapet guns, showed many shot holes which entered the brick cutting out about two feet. The eastern angle was built new, having been battered down in 1862 by the Federals. About eighty shots seem to have struck the south and east walls, to the left and right of the new angle. The fort is on a low, marshy island called Cockspur Island. The great strength of the fort is in the marshy surroundings and the river, though [Gillmore]*...reduced it in one day with eleven batteries and a few gunboats. It is seventeen miles to Savannah and the Confederate lines are six miles distant.*

After its capture, Federal troops were stationed at Fort Pulaski until the end of the war. At the time of the arrival of the Morris Island prisoners, the fort was garrisoned by a New York regiment under the command of Colonel Philip Perry Brown.

According to Henry H. Cook, some of the Confederate officers made an attempt to escape upon their arrival at Fort Pulaski. Their attempt was unsuccessful, but as it turned out, all the prisoners were pleasantly surprised by the conditions they found there. Cook wrote:

We reached Fort Pulaski about midnight, and while at anchor several of the party made a most reckless attempt to escape. During the passage down some of them had cut a hole in the stern of the vessel, and when we reached anchor six or seven lowered themselves into the water. They were soon discovered, fished out, and brought back into the ship. It would have been impossible for them to escape, as there are nothing but little barren islands on the coast, and had they reached these they would have starved to death. The mainland was too far off to be reached.

The next morning we landed and were conducted to the interior of the fort…The following morning we met Col. P.P. Brown, Lieut.-Col. Carmichael, and many of the One Hundred and Fifty-seventh New York Regiment. Never during the war did I meet better looking and better disciplined or a kinder Federal regiment of men. Col. Brown addressed us in a kind manner. He promised all in his power for our comfort, not contrary to orders from headquarters…Provisions were supplied in quantity and quality as good as we could reasonably expect, and we began to improve in health and appearance.

The prisoners were held within the fort's casemates, the open windows of which were barred by an iron grating. These brick chambers with high vaulted ceilings had once housed cannons but were now adapted for use as a prison. John Ogden Murray remembered their quarters and first hours at Fort Pulaski:

[We] were marched into the fort casemates, on the north side of the fort. Here we found luxurious quarters, consisting of rough pine board bunks to hold four people—two on top, two below,—no stoves, no blankets, no comforts, but the hard, rough pine board bunks; no downy pillow; no good, thick, warm comforts; no washstands, no easy rockers. All was hard, rough pine board bunks, and some of our fellows had the temerity to openly complain of such winter quarters, and say ugly things of the best government, etc., etc., while others thanked God we had white troops as guards. Our first meal in Fort Pulaski was a feast fit for the gods. It consisted of excellent white bread, good fat meat, and a great big tin of delicious vegetable soup, with lots of grease in it. After getting settled in the fort, with splendid cisterns of good drinking water, we began to think our troubles and woes had ended.

Col. P.P. Brown, commandant of Fort Pulaski…came into our prison quarters. We were drawn up in line, and he made a short speech. He said:

"Gentlemen, you shall be treated, while in my custody, humanely. You who have friends within our lines with whom you can correspond may write them at once for money, clothing, and other such articles that will add to your comfort. I will do all for you I can do, consistent with my duty, to make you as comfortable as possible. Myself and my regiment have seen service in the field and know what is due a brave foe. I will make this the model military prison of the United States. I have already made requisition on headquarters for blankets and clothing for you, and full army rations, together with plenty of fuel. All I shall ask is that you obey orders for government of the prison, and such sanitary rules as shall be issued by me."

We began to believe this was a dream...But, alas, we were to be rudely awakened from this happy dream.

The Confederate officers settled into their new quarters, many of them hoping that their stay at Fort Pulaski would be a short one and that there was now some prospect of exchange. Writing in his diary in early November, Captain Dickinson commented on the presidential election going on in the Northern states that ultimately resulted in Abraham Lincoln's second term:

This day is the United States vote for president. At this place there is no voting. The One Hundred and Fifty-seventh New York have voted some time since and sent their ballots on. I heard two of the privates talking today. One said he wished he was at home to vote for McClellan; the other said he tried to vote for McClellan but they found out how he intended to vote and, because he was under twenty-one when he enlisted, they told him they reckoned he didn't have a vote. Such a farce of an election.

In Georgia, the winter of 1864 was severe. Colonel Brown's requisition for blankets was never fulfilled, and as the season wore on, a number of the prisoners suffered for it. In his diary entry for November 27, Lieutenant William E. Johnson noted that the weather had been very cold for several days and that many men were without blankets.

Four stoves were installed in the prison barracks in early November, and the Confederate officers were required to do their own cooking on them. Each morning, the prisoners were issued their food rations, and they were also allowed to supplement their diet with packages received from the outside and purchases from the prison sutler. John Ogden Murray gave details about their life at Fort Pulaski during this time:

Each man was his own cook. In the casemate of each division of prisoners there was a very large cook stove; each twenty-four hours twelve cords sticks of wood—pine—was issued to each twenty-eight men or division, as they were designated. The fires were started in the cook stoves but once each day—at noon—so that the prisoner who was not ready to cook his meal when the fire was started, ate it raw or let it alone until noon next day, when the fire would again be started…

There was no fuel allowed to us for fires during the day, yet some of our men would manage to get hold of a chunk of coal, and, with an old camp kettle, they constructed stoves, and kept the atmosphere just above the freezing point…On Christmas day, 1864, the snow on the parade ground was four inches deep.

Captain George W. Nelson also recounted the sufferings of the poorly clad prisoners during the bitterly cold weather:

Our poor fellows generally were supplied, and that slimly, with summer clothing, such as they had brought from Fort Delaware in August. United States blankets (and many had no other kind) had been taken away at Morris Island…We had only so much fuel as was needed for cooking. Can a more miserable state of existence be imagined than this?

Many men grew ill in the damp, freezing casemates, suffering from bronchitis, dysentery, pneumonia and scurvy, and under a policy of retaliation, the prison doctor was not allowed to give them any medicine except painkillers, principally opiates. Some of the sick prisoners became addicted to opium; one in particular was the pathetic case of Captain George B. Fitzgerald, known as "Fitz." Captain Henry Dickinson tried to help this officer, writing of him in his diary:

Today Lieutenant Handley, myself and others endeavored to raise a small fund to buy clothes and some food for…Captain Fitzgerald, a poor, old, opium-eating, lousy inebriate, who has seen better days. He is a graduate of West Point, but has sunk in the scale till he is an object of great pity. He has no blankets, no shirt, pants filthy and worn out, is sick and cries out to every man who passes him to give him opium. We raised a small

Casemates in Fort Pulaski were adapted for use as a prison in 1864. This photograph was taken circa 1940. *Library of Congress.*

fund. Lieutenant Hassie's subscription to the fund was $4.00; Captain Bailey's, $1.00, and Lieutenant Handley's, 25c, and I am disbursing agent. I gave Lieutenant Handley $5.00 to buy pants…Poor old "Fitz" is so filthy and lousy they won't receive him in the hospital. A number of men report that they have pains in their bowels that they may get opium for old Fitz.

Soon after this was written, Dickinson recorded the death of Captain Fitzgerald:

[T]his morning announcement was made that "Fitz is dead." He was a confirmed opium eater; a poor, miserable wreck—ragged, filthy, lousy, loathed by all, and pitied by many, who reported sick that they might get opium for him. He has had no blanket, no socks, hardly clothes to cover him; none of us could supply him, and he slept alone, covering himself

with an old piece of tent fly. It was known that he was threatened with pneumonia, but the doctor didn't want him at the hospital and wouldn't take him till Lieutenant Finley, myself and others repeatedly insisted. Upon inquiring I find that he was found dead in his bed this morning. Might not a coroner's jury say that he died from neglect? Poor man! Once he had all the comforts wealth could give him. A graduate of West Point; a lieutenant in the old army, mingling with the Lees, McCllellands and Grants…Today Lieutenant-Colonel Christian, Lieutenant Finley, myself and two other officers attended his remains to the grave, because he was a Southern man, for we knew him only as "Fitz" and he had no friends. The Yanks gave us a military escort and buried him decently.

According to John Ogden Murray, "About December 10th scurvy made its appearance in our prison among the weakest of the prisoners." Captain Henry C. Dickinson's diary recorded cases of scurvy as early as the first part of November. "I have been sick for days with diarrhea and scurvy, but going about," he wrote on the tenth of that month. "Many have the scurvy." On November 12, Dickinson estimated that one hundred men were afflicted with this condition.

Later in November, Colonel Brown determined that the prison at Fort Pulaski was too crowded, and consequently, nearly two hundred of the Confederate officers were removed and sent to a prison on Hilton Head Island, South Carolina, where they would first be kept, as Captain John L. Dunkle described it, "in a square enclosure on the beach." These prisoners would also share in the same sufferings and deprivations that were soon to come upon their comrades who remained at Fort Pulaski.

Lieutenant Peter B. Akers of Virginia was one of the officers removed to Hilton Head in November 1864. In a memoir, he recalled that their first week there was spent at "a camp a mile in rear of Hilton Head village," where the headquarters of the military department commanded by General John G. Foster was located. According to Akers, during this time, the Hilton Head prisoners were housed very uncomfortably "in old A-tents we used on Morris Island." He went on to say, "At the end of the week we were removed from the canvas city into a large log building in the town of Hilton Head. This log house was built and used by the United States government as a military prison for the Department of the South, to confine the white and negro Yankee deserters, oath-takers, murderers, thieves, and all the camp-following villains of the United States army."

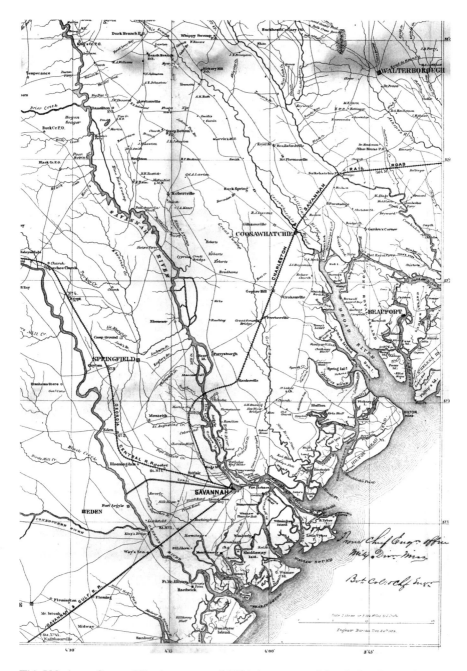

This U.S. Army Corps of Engineers map of 1864 shows parts of South Carolina and Georgia, including Hilton Head Island, Savannah and Tybee Island. The site of Fort Pulaski is also marked. *Library of Congress.*

In early December, a few Confederate officers at Fort Pulaski were chosen for exchange and taken to Charleston, with thirty more following toward the middle of the month. Captain Thomas Pinckney was one of these fortunate men.

On December 4, Captain Henry C. Dickinson was one of seventy-five prisoners who attended a religious service at Fort Pulaski, an experience he found very distasteful:

> *The prayer asked for victory over our enemies, blessings on our president and all other rulers and generals and for a "united land." Some* [of the prisoners], *who were reverently standing, sat down when this was uttered, and I felt like leaving, but, being under guard, couldn't without kicking up a row, so like an old Virginian, I went to whittling. The sermon preached to the Yanks had one virtue—it was short. The text was "What advantage a man if he gain the whole world and lose," etc. From this text the preacher of God's word deduced political conclusions, and fully compared the rebellion against his government to the rebellion of the sinner against the Most High. This puppy is, I expect, the best type of a Northern Christian! They hate the government and the bible; all else must bend to centralized power and abolitionism.*

As the days wore on and more of the Fort Pulaski prisoners grew sick and disabled, some compassionate officers who wished to help them formed a relief association, of which Murray wrote:

> *We who were true can speak of the comradeship of love to each other. It was born in suffering, cemented by the brutality of a civilized government controlled by brutes. Men, as a rule, when suffering, become selfish; but this was not true of the majority of the six hundred. Of course, there were some selfish men in our number, but it can be truthfully said…that there never was a grander lot of men brought together than the Immortal Six Hundred. The efforts of one prisoner to relieve the other were sublime.*

At a meeting held on December 13, 1864, a group of officers drew up a constitution for "The Confederate Relief Association." Its preamble stated that "a number of our brother officers, confined with us as prisoners of war at Fort Pulaski, are deprived of some absolute necessaries of life, by reason of their inability to communicate with their homes and friends," and that "some of such officers, by reason of the diseases incident to prison life, are exposed to much suffering and in danger of neglect." The officers forming the association recognized "the binding obligation on us, as Confederate officers, to search for and relieve the distress of all worthy officers and soldiers of our common country."

On December 21, surprising and extremely discouraging news was given to the prisoners, as Captain Dickinson recorded in disbelief: "The day was quite cold and windy, and many said it was a very long one. At sunset there were unmistakable signs that the Yanks had good news. Presently the band began to play, three cheers were given and they soon brought us news that Savannah had fallen. They say…that the city fell at 5 o'clock this morning…We can't believe this. It seems preposterous."

After a destructive march across the state of Georgia, General William T. Sherman's army now occupied the city of Savannah, a fact that further disheartened the Fort Pulaski prisoners, who passed a bitterly cold Christmas season. John Ogden Murray, who recalled that Christmas Eve was one of the coldest nights they had suffered so far, began to feel so despondent and miserable that he wanted to die. Something happened that night, however, that restored some hope to him:

> I was lying in my bunk, praying that God would let me go to sleep and never awake in life. Yes, I was begging God to let me die and end my torture. I was cold and hungry, no blanket to cover me, no fire to warm me. As I turned over in my bunk, to warm the side of my body exposed to the cold, one of the boards fell from the bunk, and I got out to replace it, that I might lie down. In fixing the board in its place, by the dim light of the prison lamp, I saw beneath my bunk a trap door. For a few moments I felt dazed and really believed I was dreaming. After a little while I gathered my wits, and this thought came to me: "Providence has answered your prayer; through this door you can reach liberty."

The trapdoor Murray had discovered opened into a kind of basement chamber filled with water and mud. Beginning on Christmas night, Murray and other prisoners began an effort to cut a tunnel through a brick foundation wall of the fort in that chamber. They worked persistently until February 28, 1865, and that night went through the tunnel, which led to another casemate that was not part of the prison, going up into it through another trapdoor that led up into the quartermaster's department. There they escaped through the casemate window, lowering themselves down outside on a rope made of rags and blankets. The prisoners made their way to the wharf, where they hoped to steal a boat for their getaway, but just as two of them were about to seize the sentinel posted there, a prisoner named Gillespie lost his nerve and shouted out for the guard not to shoot. All hope of escape was lost as other garrison soldiers were alerted by his cries. As punishment, the would-be escapees were manacled and put in close confinement for five days.

Chapter 4

Retaliatory Ordeal at Fort Pulaski

Some of the grateful Confederate officers who had been exchanged in early December published a letter to Colonel Brown in a Charleston newspaper, thanking him for the humane treatment he had accorded the Fort Pulaski prisoners. The letter, printed in the *Charleston Daily Courier* on December 7, 1864, read in part:

> *In a few hours we will be free. We wish to anticipate that wished for moment, and before we land to leave you the freely spoken expressions of our respect for you and the lively sense of gratitude with which we will ever remember your kindness.*
>
> *During the time we have remained prisoners in your hands you have clearly demonstrated the truth of the oft forgotten principle, that duty can always be made compatible with humanity; and while enforcing strictly measures necessary for our safe-keeping, you have invariably shown us the courtesy of a gallant soldier and Christian gentleman.*

Unfortunately, the gesture of appreciation offered by these men would bring about bitter consequences for their fellow officers still confined at Fort Pulaski. When this letter came to the attention of General John G. Foster, Brown was reprimanded for his leniency with the prisoners and was ordered to cut their ration of meat and put an end to their sutler privileges.

At the end of December, Colonel Brown was compelled to enforce even harsher measures against the prisoners in his charge. This was the beginning of the retaliatory ordeal. Their rations were reduced to ten ounces of cornmeal a day per man, along with a supply of pickles. The cornmeal issued to the prisoners was several years old, rancid and infested with insects. On January 19, Captain Dickinson recorded in his diary that the rations also included a few ounces of bread.

Lieutenant Henry H. Cook described the beginning and progress of the retaliatory ordeal:

> *Col. Brown was much moved, and his voice was tremulous when he informed us of the new orders, but he attempted to cheer us, stating that he hoped the cruel treatment would be of short duration. Winter had now fairly set in, and its chilly blasts off the Atlantic wailed mournfully through our open casemate windows, causing the poorly clad prisoners to shiver. It was a damp, nipping, and eager cold, such as no one who experienced it could soon forget.*
>
> *Our supply of wood had also been cut off to barely enough to cook our small supply of rotten cornmeal. Through the whole winter we knew not what it was to feel the warmth of fire. The officers were poorly clad, many of them not having blankets… The casemates were damp and the brick floor was at all times wet, as if it had been rained upon. We paced the vaults to keep warm. Some would walk while some slept, and thus the time passed slowly away. Day after day and week after week passed.*
>
> *In a short time our treatment began to tell fearfully. The officers of the garrison hid themselves from us, and were seldom seen, and the privates were only seen on their posts of duty. The New York Regiment, officers and privates, were a noble set of men, and were manifestly pained at our plight when they came into our prison.*

Captain George W. Nelson recalled:

> *The new year brought a terrible change. General Foster ordered us to be retaliated upon for alleged ill treatment of prisoners at Andersonville, Georgia. Our rations were reduced to less than one pint of meal and about a half pint of pickle per day. No meat and no vegetables of any kind were allowed us. The meal issued was damaged. It was in lumps larger than a man's head, and as hard as clay: it was sour, and generally filled with bugs and worms. We either had to eat this or lie down and die at once. This regimen lasted forty-three days.*

According to Colonel Abram Fulkerson, the acidic pickles were mostly rejected when it was discovered that they did more harm than good. "The effect of the pickle," he wrote, "was to thin the blood, and its use was quickly abandoned by the prisoners."

The prisoners on Hilton Head Island were also subjected to the same meager rations. Lieutenant Peter B. Akers recounted their sufferings:

The rations for the first week of our sojourn at Hilton Head were first class. But after that week, it was followed by the delicious, the palatable, and strength destroying ration of rotten corn meal and one-half pint of cucumber and onion pickle, without salt or grease of any kind—all we got was rotten corn meal and pickle. It now began to dawn upon our minds that we were, sure enough, General Foster's victims. After ten days on the corn meal diet, our condition was horrible. Col. Van Manning made a personal protest, against this cruelty and rations, to Colonel Gurney, the provost-marshal in charge of our prison, and made a written protest to General Foster; but the ration of corn meal was not changed, nor the cruelty of Foster in the least abated…It is a great pity that those artists of the North, who from their fertile brains created pictures of the woe and suffering of Yankee prisoners of war in the prisons of the South, let our Hilton Head prison escape their lurid pencils. What grand subjects of suffering they could have drawn from our condition in that prison. Yea, they would have found much to depict to their readers in the North, and much, indeed, to make them hide their heads in shame at the slanders they wrote against the South and our people. To misstate the facts, to slander the South, and vilify President Davis, seemed to be, during the war of 1861–65, the only mission of the Yankee artist. It fired the Northern heart; it brought new recruits to the army of coercion…

It was a brutal mind that conceived the corn meal and pickle diet…On this diet of corn meal, with no meat or vegetables, scurvy soon came to add to our suffering, and acute dysentery was prevalent among our men…The pangs of starvation became terrible; hunger drove our men to catching and eating dogs, cats, and rats. It was dainty food to starving men.

According to the diary of Captain Henry Dickinson, the retaliation diet of rotten cornmeal and pickles at Fort Pulaski began on December 31, 1864, a day he described as a "raw, cold, drizzling day, and one of damp gloom to all."

The threatened ration is at last issued! Ten barrels of corn meal—funky, wormy, and sour, and two and one-half kegs of mean pickles with a little, very little, salt, are ten days' rations for 313 men. No meat, no vegetables—nothing but sour meal and pickles. And this food for men fully one-half of whom have diseased bowels! Well may we be gloomy, for a few weeks at most will terribly thin our ranks. All, however, evince a determination to bear it as long as they can.

John Ogden Murray added the following details:

Brown was ordered to issue to us ten ounces of corn meal and one-half pint of onion pickle each twenty-four hours, as a ration, without salt, meat, grease, or vegetables….No fuel but twelve sticks of pine cord wood for each division of twenty-eight men. The order, he said, was peremptory, leaving him no discretion whatever, and he was powerless in the matter. It must be said of Colonel Brown and his officers that they were gentlemen, and when he made the promise to treat us humanely and kindly he intended to keep his promise to the letter. The officers and men of the 157th New York never failed to show their disgust for General Foster and his brutal corn meal order…If the corn meal had been good we might have managed to live upon it and kept off the scurvy; but the meal was rotten—filled with black weevil bugs and worms. The barrels were branded, "Corn meal, kiln dried from —— Mills, 1861," showing by the brand and date on the barrels that it was four years old…After picking out the lumps, bugs, and worms in this rotten corn meal there was not more than seven ounces of meal left for use.

Many of the prisoners at Fort Pulaski chronicled the results of General Foster's orders. Colonel Abram Fulkerson recalled how the prisoners tried to supplement their diet:

The prisoners' quarters were separate from the casemates occupied by the soldiers of the garrison by a kind of grate made of heavy iron bars. The soldiers of the garrison had a great number of cats; indeed, every soldier seemed to have his pet. The cats had free access to our quarters through the iron grating, and being gentle and friendly disposed, they were given a warm reception by the prisoners. Not a great while after we were put on retaliation rations, some enterprising or half-starved prisoners conceived the happy idea of testing cat flesh as an article of food. The experiment proved a success, and thereafter cats rapidly disappeared. The cats were generally captured, killed and dressed during the night. The soldiers were at a loss to know what had become of their pets, but they soon discovered the skins floating in the moat, and this led to the discovery that prisoners were killing them for food. Some complaint was made to Colonel Brown, but to no purpose. The Colonel himself had a fine pet, which he prized very highly, and when he heard of the havoc among the garrison cats, he came into the prison one day and made a special request that his cat be spared. Of course his request was respected by every one of the prisoners, and thereafter his pet had the liberty of the prison, day and night, without even the fear of molestation.

On January 6, Henry C. Dickinson noted in his diary that the retaliation diet was already "telling on the more delicate." Two days later, he wrote:

We suffered terribly today; the weather was very cold and damp, with an east wind. All who can have wrapped up in blankets. The coughing and limping continues. No wood was furnished us, and as a consequence we shall not be able to cook our sour meal tomorrow. Somehow, the supply of wood is shortest on cold days. A few men, some three or four messes, can still eat meat bought from the sutlery at forty cents. Whilst it is being cooked, many a mouth waters. Last night two cats were captured and to my surprise were eaten today.

In his diary entry of January 8, 1865, Lieutenant William E. Johnson remarked that he had observed some officers eating a fried cat and that it looked fat and tasty. Captain George W. Nelson was one of the prisoners who partook of feline flesh on several occasions:

Fortunately for some of us, there were a great many cats about the prison. As may be imagined, we were glad enough to eat them. I have been a partner in the killing and eating of three, and besides friends have frequently given me a share of their cat. We cooked ours two ways. One we fried in his own fat for breakfast—another we baked with a stuffing and gravy made of some corn meal—the other we also fried. The last was a kitten— tender and nice. A compassionate Yankee soldier gave it to me. I was cooking at the stove by the grating which separated us from the guard. This soldier hailed me: "I say, are you one of them fellers that eat cats?" I replied, "Yes." "Well, here is one I'll shove thro' if you want

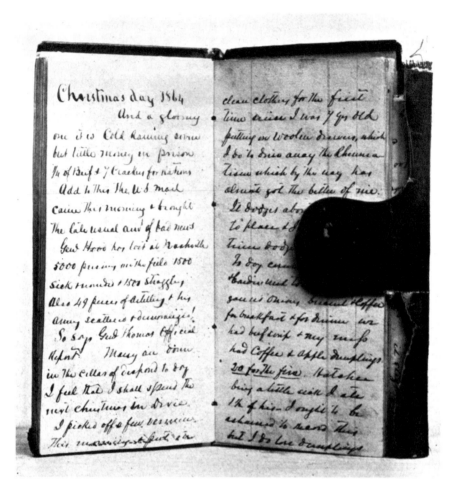

One of the diaries of Captain Henry C. Dickinson, opened to an entry that begins on December 25, 1864, just days before the retaliation ordeal began at Fort Pulaski. Captain Dickinson died in 1871, and many years later, one of his daughters transcribed the diary (written in five small memorandum books like this one) and published it as "an exact copy." *From the collections of the South Carolina Historical Society.*

it." "Shove it thro,'" I answered. In a very few minutes the kitten was in frying order.

Another prisoner, Lieutenant William W. George of Virginia, recalled the day he spied a "large cat" under one of the casemate stoves:

There were, perhaps, as many as forty-seven or fifty of these cats making their home in the fort. The thought came quickly—"I will prepare one of these for dinner tomorrow." I had never tasted cat's flesh, but I fancied it might be palatable, especially to hungry men.

Immediately I caught the cat, held in my left hand by the back of its neck, and with a stick held in the right hand, soon dispatched it with a few strong blows. It was carefully dressed, parboiled, and baked in a pan in our prison stove. While I was thus engaged, the officer of the day made his appearance, and asked me what I was doing. I suppose his astonishment prompted the question. I replied I was killing a cat, and when he inquired what I intended to do with it, I said, "Eat it," and invited him to dine with our mess next day.

He declined with thanks, and at the same time expressed his sympathy, and regretted that the prisoners had to resort to such means to satisfy hunger.

As Captain Dickinson noted in his diary on January 8, those who had the means could still buy food from the sutler (a privilege that Colonel Brown had apparently restored at some point), but few of the prisoners were fortunate enough to have any money left. On January 19, Dickinson wrote: "The ration continues to be four ounces bread and three fourths of a pint of sour meal, without salt, vinegar, vegetables, meat or anything but water. All complain among ourselves, but observe silence in the presence of the enemy. Very few men have any money, and those few find it hard to stand up to [the sutler's] prices."

As the days went by, the suffering of the prisoners worsened. Within a month after the reduction in rations, Henry E. Handerson recalled, the sick list assumed "alarming proportions." John Ogden Murray described the effects of the starvation diet imposed on the Fort Pulaski prisoners:

Hunger drove our men to catching and eating dogs, cats, and rats…On the first day of January, 1865, the scurvy became prevalent in our prison. The doctor, whose name I cannot remember, did the best he could for us with the medicine General Foster's order allowed him to use in practice amongst the prisoners. He would often say, "Men, the medicines allowed me are not the proper remedies for scurvy, but I can get no other for you."

There were remedies called antiscorbutics the physician could have given to the officers suffering from scurvy, but because medicines were insufficient in Confederate prisons for Union prisoners of war, he was forbidden from prescribing them to the Fort Pulaski prisoners—this despite the fact that many of these shortages could be attributed to the United States government, which, at the beginning of the war, had declared certain medicines and medical supplies contraband.

After the war, Captain Henry Wirz, the commandant of Andersonville prison camp in Georgia, was put on trial for war crimes by the United States government, accused of deliberate mistreatment of the prisoners there. In 1867, Louis F. Schade, a Washington attorney who defended Wirz and steadfastly maintained that the captain was innocent of these charges, wrote a letter that sheds light on the reasons for the mortality and shortages of medicines in Southern prisons in 1864:

> But who is responsible for the many lives that were lost at Andersonville, and in the Southern prisons?...It was certainly not the fault of poor Captain Wirz, when, in consequence of medicines having been declared contraband of war by the North, the Union prisoners died for want of the same...Our navy prevented the ingress of medical stores from the sea-side, and our troops repeatedly destroyed drug stores, and even the supplies of private physicians in the South. Thus, the scarcity of medicines became general all over the South. Surgeon J.C. Pilot writes, September 6th, 1864, from Andersonville, (this letter was produced by the Judge Advocate in the Wirz trial): "We have little more than the indigenous barks and roots with which to treat the numerous forms of disease to which our attention is daily called. For the treatment of wounds, ulcers, &c., we have literally nothing, except water."
>
> That provisions in the South were scarce, will astonish nobody, when it is remembered how the war was carried on. General Sheridan boasted, in his official report that, in the Shenandoah valley alone, he burned two thousand barns filled with wheat and corn, and all the mills in the whole tract of country; that he destroyed the factories of cloth, and killed, or drove off, every animal, even to the poultry, that could contribute to human sustenance. And those desolations were repeated in different parts of the South, and that so thoroughly, that last month, two years after the end of the war, Congress had to appropriate a million of dollars, to save the people of those regions from actual starvation. The destruction of railroads, and other means of transportation, by which food should be supplied by abundant districts to those without it, increased the difficulties in giving sufficient food to our prisoners.

The Confederate authorities, aware of their inability to maintain the prisoners, informed the Northern agents of the great mortality, and urgently requested that the prisoners should be exchanged, even without regard to the surplus which the Confederates had on the exchange roll from former exchanges, that is, man for man, but our War Department did not consent to an exchange. They did not want to "exchange skeletons for healthy men." Finally, when all hopes of exchange were gone, Colonel Ould, the Confederate Commissioner, offered, early in August 1864, to deliver up all the Federal sick and wounded, without requiring an equivalent in return, and pledged that the number would amount to ten or fifteen thousand, and, that if it did not, he would make up that number with well men. Although this offer was made in August, the transportation was not sent for them (to Savannah) until December, although he urged and implored (to use his own words) that haste should be made. During that very period, most of the deaths at Andersonville occurred.

Deprived of any remedies for scurvy, the prisoners at Fort Pulaski observed the dreaded condition spreading through their ranks. Lieutenant Henry H. Cook wrote:

If our condition was horrible on Morris Island, it was much more so here. Many were unable to walk; others meandered through the vaults like living skeletons, gazing into each others' faces with a listless, vacant stare, plainly indicating that they were bordering upon imbecility or lunacy. That dreadful disease, the scurvy, was raging fearfully, so that the mouths were in a fearful condition, their gums decaying and sloughing off and their teeth falling out; while others had the disease in a more dangerous form, their arms and legs swelling, mortifying, and becoming black. Black spots appeared upon the arms and legs of some, looking as though the veins and arteries had decomposed, separated, and spilled the blood in the flesh. One day when some of our dead were carried over to the graveyard Col. Brown had a military salute fired over their graves, but this was soon forbidden, and then, day by day, the dead were silently and sadly carried and laid in their graves.

All of us knew full well that unless relief soon came we must soon pass out at the Sally Port, now the funeral arch to the graveyard.

Captain George W. Nelson's description of the effects of the scurvy was very similar to that of Lieutenant Cook:

Our diet soon induced scurvy. This loathesome disease, in addition to the pangs of hunger, made life almost insupportable. The disease first made its appearance in the mouth, loosening the teeth, and in many cases making the gums a mass of black, putrid flesh. It next attacked the limbs, appearing first in little spots, like blood blisters. One of them, after being broken, would become a hard, dark-colored knot. These spots would increase until the whole limb was covered, by which time the muscles would have contracted and the limb be drawn beyond all power of straightening…Another feature of the disease was the fainting produced by very slight exercise. I have walked down the prison, and stumbled upon men lying on the floor to all appearances dead, having fainted and fallen while exerting themselves to get to the "sinks."

Captain Nelson also wrote of the deaths that began to occur among the Fort Pulaski prisoners because of exposure and malnutrition:

Starved almost to the point of death, a prey to disease, the blood in the veins so thin that the least cold sent a shiver through the whole frame! No fire, no blankets, scarcely any clothing! Add to this the knowledge on our part that a few steps off were those who lived in plenty and comfort! Crumbs and bones were there daily thrown to the dogs or carried to the dunghill, that would have made the eyes of famished men in that prison glisten. Whatever the immediate cause of their death, that cause was induced by starvation, and over the dead bodies of nine-tenths of those brave, true men there can be given but one true verdict: "Death by starvation." I remember one instance that, suffering as I was myself, touched me to the heart. One poor fellow, who had grown so weak as not to be able to get off his bunk, said to his "chum": "I can't stand this any longer, I must die." "O, no," said the other, "cheer up, man, rations will be issued again in two days, and I reckon they will certainly give us something to eat then—live until then anyhow." The poor fellow continued to live until the day for issuing rations, but it brought no change—the same short pint of damaged meal and pickle, and nothing more. As soon as the poor fellow heard this, he told his friend not to beg him anymore, for he could not live any longer, and the next evening, he died.

Lieutenant Henry H. Cook recorded that, in the latter part of January, Colonel Brown went to Savannah and returned to Fort Pulaski

A view of the Fort Pulaski parade ground and casemates. This photograph was taken in the twentieth century. *Library of Congress.*

with "five or six medical officers, who went through the prison and made a close inspection."

> *When they came to my bunk I was nursing…several other officers who were unable to walk or assist themselves in any way. I myself was able to stand up and walk for a few minutes at a time. I asked them why medical officers should come into the prison, and one of them replied, "We wish to see how much longer you can live under this treatment." Of course I was displeased at this apparently flippant and heartless remark, but I learned from others that the inspectors were really kind and humane, and were shocked and horrified at our condition. One of them stated that he would not have believed a Federal officer guilty of such horrible brutality if he had not seen it himself. One stated that in all his experience he had never seen a place so horrible or known of men being treated with such brutality.*

On the first day of February, Lieutenant William E. Johnson recorded in his diary that many of the prisoners were very ill and that they would die soon unless provided with better food. On that same day, in his diary, Captain Henry C. Dickinson noted, "Our sick list has increased to a terrible extent," adding:

> We hear no rumors of improved diet and still have the pickles and sour corn meal. Cats can no longer be gotten. None of us have any money. Neither money nor clothes are allowed to come in, and we are in a deplorable fix…I must express the opinion that no prisoners in a civilized country ever received more barbarous treatment than we have for the last thirty days.

John Ogden Murray recalled that during the last days of January, "Our condition was almost beyond endurance." Years after the war, in the U.S. government's *Official Records*, Murray found a letter that had been written by General Grover, the Union officer in command of the District of Savannah, concerning the condition of the Fort Pulaski prisoners. Addressed to the assistant adjutant general and dated February 7, 1865, it read in part:

> My medical director yesterday inspected the condition of the Rebel prisoners confined at Fort Pulaski, and represents that they are in a condition of great suffering and exhaustion for want of sufficient food and clothing; also, that they have scurvy to a considerable extent. He recommends, as a necessary sanitary measure, that they be at once put on full prison rations and, also, that they be allowed to receive necessary articles of clothing from friends. I would respectfully endorse the surgeon's recommendations, and ask authority to take such steps as may be necessary to relieve actual sickness and suffering.

According to Murray, "No attention was paid by headquarters to this request of General Grover." Murray recorded, however, that the prisoners did receive some help at times from the soldiers of the prison garrison:

> There were lots of good fellows in the….New York Volunteers. They had been often under fire, and could appreciate the condition and feel for the prisoners of war. Often, when they were on duty about the prison some of them would put a loaf of bread or piece of meat on the end of their bayonets and dare any Rebel to take it off, always holding their guns in such position that the meat or bread could be taken off by the prisoners.

These men took this method of helping us and getting around the orders. They dare not openly disobey. There was one officer in this regiment who deserves well of every Fort Pulaski prisoner. He was Major Place, quartermaster of the post. His kindness to the prisoners will ever be remembered by us all of the Fort Pulaski detachment. On one occasion this kind hearted fellow took a lot of his men fishing with seines in the Savannah River about the fort. At night, after their return, Major Place gave Capt. Ed. Chambers, of Alabama, one of the prisoners, a barrel of the fish he and his men had caught during the day. "These," he said, "Captain Chambers, distribute to your sick men who cannot get about." At another time he gave Captain Chambers a half-barrel of damaged coffee, which had been condemned by the quartermaster department, and would have been thrown out…God bless you, Major Place! May you prosper in this world, and the world to come, for your goodness and humanity to our starving men.

Murray also related the story of "one of the very sad cases of the regime at Fort Pulaski."

Lieut. Billy Funk, 5th Regt., Stonewall Brigade, one of our number, was little more than a boy in years when he joined the Confederate Army in 1861. A gallant, brave boy, he was captured May 12, 1864, at the battle of Spotsylvania Court House, reaching Fort Delaware prison just in time to be selected as one of the six hundred to be turned over to the tender care of…Gen. J.G. Foster, U.S.A. Upon Lieutenant Funk the rigors of retaliation worked very hard, and soon completely broke him down. But never a complaint escaped his lips, and he bore his suffering like a hero. Lieut. Tom S. Doyle, a noble fellow, Funk's messmate and regimental comrade, with us all, did all we could to help him and keep him alive, giving him part of our scanty corn meal ration and all the white bread given us, which was just two ounces… In his suffering with dysentery and scurvy Funk lost heart and nerve, slowly starving to death. One day I had the good fortune to catch a big fat cat. Capt. Thornton Hammack, 49th Ky. Regt., skinned the animal for me, and dressed it for the pan. In an old tin can I made soup of part of the cat for Funk, and, after threats and coaxing, I prevailed upon him to drink some of the soup. The effect upon him was magical. It revived him in spirits and for a time counteracted the effects of the scurvy. As long as I could get him rat and cat meat he showed signs of improvement; but the cats gave out, and the rats I could not catch. I had not the wealth to purchase them from the fellows who could, so poor Billy Funk relapsed back into his former condition. He never rallied, and died, shortly after our return to Fort Delaware prison, in the arms of his mother who was allowed to see him an hour or two before his death.

On February 6, 1865, Captain Henry C. Dickinson recorded a list of the sick in his diary:

By the suggestion of several friends I procured a list of the sick in prison. All data except the classification of diseases is correct. A number, who at home or in the army would be considered sick, are classed as well. Indeed there are not twenty men in the whole prison who are able to do military duty; all are poor, shriveled remnants of humanity.

According to Dickinson's list, of the 311 prisoners at Fort Pulaski, 156 were classified as sick. Those afflicted with scurvy numbered 42; those with chronic diarrhea and dysentery, 37; and another 43 men suffered with "coughs and diseases of throat." Some suffered with "acute rheumatism" and other diseases, and 8 men were listed as "very sick at hospital."

In the middle of February 1865, the retaliation regime finally ended, and the Fort Pulaski prisoners began receiving much better rations. In his diary entry of February 15, Henry C. Dickinson recorded, "Our new ration was issued to us today." At Hilton Head, according to Lieutenant Peter B. Akers's memoir, orders emanating from the Department of the South were posted on February 7 directing the addition of "four ounces of meat per diem" and "four ounces of potatoes." Akers recalled that the order "brought joy to our hearts. Four ounces of meat and four ounces of potatoes to be added to our corn meal diet! It would save us from death." Another Hilton Head prisoner, William Epps, recorded in his diary that some meat and potatoes were issued a little earlier, on January 27, and that "full rations" were issued on February 20. Earlier, in December 1864, Epps recorded that the "Yanks" said they were retaliating against the Confederate prisoners because of the mistreatment of Union prisoners in Columbia, South Carolina. Some of these Union prisoners had escaped and made their way to Hilton Head, but they gave contradictory reports of their treatment at Columbia.

Soon after the improvement in rations for the prisoners at Fort Pulaski, the New York regiment under the command of Colonel Brown was replaced by another garrison, a detachment from the 159th New York Volunteer Infantry commanded by Colonel Edward L. Molineaux. Toward the end of the month, the Confederate officers were once again informed that an exchange was in the offing. Lieutenant Henry H. Cook recalled:

> *About the first of March we heard that we were to be exchanged, and were directed to be in readiness to leave at any time. We were satisfied that the orders had been received, as the officers and men came among us and offered the oath of allegiance to those who wished to remain in the United States until the close of the war. I heard that five or six accepted the offer…It was on the morning of March 4, 1865, that…Molineaux entered the prison and informed us that orders had been received to send us to the James River to be exchanged. We made ready to leave the fort, but were almost unwilling to leave, notwithstanding the fact that it had been to us the scene of so much sorrow and affliction. About it lay the remains of those who were dear to us, who had died from starvation.*

During their incarceration in Georgia, thirteen of the Confederate officers died and were buried outside the walls of Fort Pulaski. Despite all the terrible hardships they endured in that place, however, most of the officers refused to take the oath of allegiance to the United States, an act that would have lessened their sufferings and deprivations and afforded them a better chance of survival.

Chapter 5

Return to Fort Delaware

Captain George W. Nelson described the departure of the prisoners from Fort Pulaski and the beginning of their voyage:

The 3rd of March, 1865, dawned upon us laden with rumors of a speedy exchange. The wings of hope had been so often clipped by disappointment, one would have thought it impossible for her to rise very high. "Hope springs," etc., received no denial in our case. Each man was more or less excited…On the 4th the order came to be ready to start in two hours. Soon after one of our ranking officers was told by one of the officials that an order was just received from Grant to exchange us immediately. We were wild with hope. The chilling despair which had settled upon us for months seemed to rise at once. All were busy packing their few articles. Cheerful talk and hearty laughter was heard all through the prison. "Well, old fellow, off for Dixie at last," was said as often as one friend met another. The alacrity with which the sick and crippled dragged themselves about was wonderful. Soon the drum beat, the line was formed and the roll called. "Forward, march!" Two by two we passed through the entrance to the Fort, over the moat, and then Fort Pulaski was left behind us forever!…

We reached Hilton Head without anything remarkable happening. Then we took on our party which had been sent there at the beginning of the retaliation, or "Meal and Pickles," as we used to call it. This party had undergone the same treatment. The greeting between friends was: "How are you, old fellow, ain't dead yet? You are hard to kill." "I'm mighty glad to see you. Have some pickles—or here is some sour meal if you prefer it." The boat in which we started was now so crowded that there was not room for all to sit down. It was so overloaded, and rolled so, that the Captain refused to put to sea unless a larger ship was given to him. Accordingly we were transferred to the ship "Illinois." The sick, about half our number, occupied the lower deck—the rest of us were packed away in the "hole." But no combination of circumstances could depress us as long as we believed we were "bound for Dixie." So we laughed at our close quarters, at ourselves and each other, when sea sick. We were almost run away with by lice, but we [took] off shirts and skirmished with these varmints with the "vim" inspired by "bound for Dixie."

There had in fact been an arrangement between General Ulysses S. Grant and the Confederate exchange agent to have some prisoners of war sent to City Point in Virginia for exchange, but for some reason, it did not include the six hundred, and when they learned that no exchange was in the works for them, most were devastated by the news. "This was disappointment's greatest shock," Colonel Abram Fulkerson recalled. "Hope, that had sustained us in every peril, now forsook us, and our hearts sank within us. All was despondency and gloom." The *Illinois* was larger than the vessel that had taken them to Hilton Head, but it was nearly as overcrowded and full of sick men, although the sickest had been left in prison hospitals.

Captain George W. Nelson added these details about the voyage:

We reached Fort Monroe on the third day. By this time the filth in the ship was awful—language can't describe the condition of the deck where the sick were. The poor fellows were unable to help themselves, and sea sickness and diarrheoa [sic] had made their quarters unendurable. The stench was terrible—the air suffocating. We expected to go right up the James river and be exchanged at City Point. We were most cruelly disappointed. Orders were received to carry us to Fort Delaware. When we learned this we were in despair. The stimulus which had enabled us to bear up all along was gone; we were utterly crushed. The deaths of three of our number during the day and night following told the tale of our utter wretchedness. Their death excited little or no pity. I think the feeling towards them was rather one of envy.

Lieutenant Henry H. Cook wrote:

We left quite a number at Pulaski and Hilton Head, who were expected to die. Being thought past all hope of recovery, they were left behind. I learned from Capt. Perkins that they [the Hilton Head prisoners] *had received about the same treatment as ourselves, and their appearance indicated the truth of his statement. He related to me that he had made his escape and had been recaptured and placed in a box or cage just large enough for him to lie down in, but not high enough to allow him to sit upright, and kept there for more than a week.*

We reached Fortress Monroe in about four days from the time we left Fort Pulaski. One of the officers died before we reached Fortress Monroe, and his remains were taken on deck, sewed up in his blanket, a heavy weight attached to sink the body, and after prayer the body was consigned to the sea. Two others died before we reached Fort Delaware.

On the 8th of March a large steamer, crowded with prisoners from Fort Delaware, passed us, bound for Richmond. They passed close enough for us to recognize each other, and many were the joyful greetings. But we did not move up the James River; hour after hour we lay at anchor. In the evening a number of medical officers came on board and went through the ship. They gave each prisoner a careful examination, and then left. We did not know the object of their visit at the time, but soon learned that we were not to be exchanged, but sent to Fort Delaware, as the medical officers had reported that our condition was so horrible that we ought not to be sent to Richmond. The ship proceeded to Norfolk to take on coal, from which place we were taken to Fort Delaware.

In his diary, Captain Henry C. Dickinson gave details about the deaths of several prisoners on board the *Illinois*. One was buried at sea just hours before the ship's arrival at its destination, an act that Dickinson considered "hasty and unnecessary." Soon afterward, a second man, Lieutenant Robert Y. Dillard, died, followed by another "whose name I did not learn," wrote Dickinson. The other prisoners covered the bodies of these two deceased individuals with blankets, concealing the corpses until the next morning.

Thus we spent the long night in the midst of disease and death, with none to pity who could relieve us. Though under the protecting care of the "best government on earth" we were only "damaged Rebels." We had withstood

103

starvation, why couldn't we still live in a crowded, filthy, reeking hole for one week? I shall never forget the night, and may I be struck dumb if I ever join hands with a nation whose agents have thus cruelly persecuted me and my friends.

The *Illinois* arrived at Fort Delaware on the morning of March 12, 1865. Upon his return there, Colonel Fulkerson observed that the prison population had grown in numbers. "They were in comparatively good health," he noted, "and the contrast between their appearance and that of the emaciated, haggard and ragged survivors of the 600 was most marked." After their harsh ordeal at Fort Pulaski, some of the surviving six hundred who were returned to Fort Delaware were in such poor physical condition that they were unrecognizable to the prisoners who had known them prior to their departure in August 1864. Writing in 1869, Captain John Dunkle recalled:

After some days sailing, we arrived safely at Fort Delaware, and were again housed in our old rooms, in the same prison from which we had gone some months ago. But oh, how changed were our faces, our countenances, and our whole frame. We exhibited the appearance of having been treated with extreme cruelty and excessive horror. Our comrades scarcely knew us, so changed were our features, and so haggard our countenances. Our number, too, was changed from what it had been…Many of us had diseases from which we never recovered. Some died in a short time, some lived longer, and some linger invalids still.

Captain George Nelson described the arrival of the prisoners at Fort Delaware and his own appearance and condition at that time:

Upon reaching Fort Delaware seventy-five of our number were carried to the prison hospital, and had there been room many more would have gone. We were marched into the same place we had left more than six months before. I had no idea what a miserable looking set of men we were until contrasted with the Fort Delaware prisoners—our old companions. I thought they were the fattest, best dressed set of men I had ever seen. That they looked thus to me, will excite no surprise when I describe my own appearance. A flannel shirt, low in the neck, was my only under-garment. An old overcoat, once white, was doing duty as a shirt, coat and vest; part of an old handkerchief tied around my head served as a hat; breeches I

Aerial view of Fort Delaware in the late twentieth century. *Library of Congress.*

had none—an antiquated pair of red flannel drawers endeavored, but with small success, to fill their place. I was very thin and poor and was lame, scurvy having drawn the muscles of my right leg. When I add that I was in better condition, both in flesh and dress than many of our crowd, some idea can be formed of the appearance we made. The prisoners came to our rescue, gave us clothes, subscribed money, and bought vegetables for us. For a long time after our arrival, whenever any one was about to throw away an old crumb or piece of meat or worn out garment, some bystander would call out: "Don't throw that away, give it to some of the poor Pulaski prisoners."

John Ogden Murray similarly described the return of a "haggard, ragged, emaciated crowd." He remembered how the Fort Delaware prisoners tried to help the unfortunate Fort Pulaski men and wished that some photographic record had been made of them.

Our comrades brought out their stores of provisions and extra clothing, giving us freely all they could spare. What a grand chance the United States Sanitary Commission missed in not having a photograph made of the survivors of Secretary Stanton's brutality…It is a pity, indeed, those loyal souls who were ever anxious to stir the Northern heart did not have taken, for distribution in the North, our photos.

Lieutenant Elijah L. Cox, a prisoner who had envied the six hundred men he saw leaving Fort Delaware in August 1864, was shocked at their condition and estimated that about sixty of the officers were taken directly to the hospital upon arrival. Robert E. Park, a prisoner who arrived at Fort Delaware in February 1865, took note of the Fort Pulaski prisoners in his diary:

These sickly, limping, miserable looking men were chosen from the prisoners last August to be…placed under fire of the Confederate batteries, in retaliation, it was said, for the placing of Federal prisoners in the city under the fire of the Yankee batteries…Their lean, emaciated persons were covered with livid spots of various sizes, occasioned by effusion of blood under the cuticle. They looked pale, languid and low spirited, and suffered from general exhaustion, pains in the limbs, and bleeding gums. All this was caused by their rigid confinement and want of nourishing food. They were not given food sufficient to supply the elements necessary to repair the natural waste of the system…The feet and legs of many were so drawn by [scurvy] as to compel them to walk on their toes, their heels being unable to touch the ground, and they used either sticks in each hand, or a rude crutch, sometimes two to aid them in hobbling along. Several, unable to walk at all, were carried on stretchers to the hospital. Our hard fare and rough treatment at Fort Delaware has been princely compared with that inflicted upon these scurvy-afflicted Fort Pulaski sufferers.

According to Mauriel P. Joslyn, author of *Immortal Captives*, forty-four of the Confederate officers taken out of Fort Delaware in August 1864 succumbed during their ordeal—five dying at Hilton Head, South Carolina, and thirteen at Fort Pulaski. The largest number died soon after their return to Fort Delaware in March 1865.

Not long after the Pulaski prisoners arrived back at Fort Delaware, the news of General Lee's surrender was announced to the Confederate prisoners of war. "The end had come," John Ogden Murray wrote, "and we were men without a country—soldiers without a flag."

Another Fort Delaware prisoner, Captain Joseph Blyth Allston from South Carolina, wrote this poem after learning of the surrender at Appomattox:

> "Stack Arms!" I've gladly heard the cry
> When, weary with the dusty tread
> Of marching troops, as night drew nigh,
> I sank upon my soldier bed,
> And calmly slept; the starry dome
> Of heaven's blue arch my canopy,
> And mingled with my dreams of home,
> The thoughts of peace and liberty.
>
> "Stack Arms!" I've heard it, when the shout
> Exulting, rang along our line,
> Of foes hurled back in bloody rout,
> Captured, dispersed; its tones divine
> They came to mine enraptured ear,
> Guerdon of duty nobly done,
> And glistened on my cheek, the tear
> Of grateful joy for victory won.
>
> "Stack Arms!" In faltering accents, slow
> And sad, it creeps from tongue to tongue,
> A broken, murmuring wail of woe,
> From manly hearts by anguish wrung.
> Like victims of a midnight dream,
> We move, we know not how nor why,
> For life and hope but phantoms seem,
> And it were a relief—to die!

These verses summed up the anguish and despair that almost every Confederate soldier must have experienced on hearing of the South's surrender after four long years of inconceivable sacrifice, tragedy and struggle. William Gilmore Simms, the famous South Carolina author, saw fit to include Allston's poem "Stack Arms!" in his *War Poetry of the South*, published in 1867.

On the first day of May 1865, Captain Henry C. Dickinson wrote that the Fort Delaware prisoners were informed of the surrender of General Joseph E. Johnston, commander of the Army of Tennessee. Dickinson and other prisoners from Virginia came together for a meeting to discuss whether they should take the oath of allegiance:

> We had just received information of the formal surrender by General Johnston of all his forces. Were we released from allegiance to the Confederate States? This question troubled many…We met at 11 a.m. on Sunday. Colonel Moseby, of Buckingham, was in the chair. Major Otey, of Lynchburg, acted as secretary. I was first called up and spoke for perhaps one-half hour. I argued that it was yet too soon to act, that the plans of Mr. Davis were not known and that he alone could release us. Captain Carrington, Captain McCue, Captain Swan, Captain Halsey, and many others followed, all thinking that the peculiar condition of Virginia demanded that we should now take the oath and go home. The meeting adjourned for dinner; in the evening I was called to the chair and our meeting opened with prayer. It was a most solemn convocation. No intemperate language was used, but real elegance, which was prompted by our hopeless condition, caused many to shed tears. I shall never forget this meeting. We passed no resolution, we left each to act for himself, but we were brought nearer together. We felt that we were brothers in adversity, and there was a tacit understanding that all of us would go home eventually and try to redeem old Virginia.
>
> On the second of May the authorities again brought in their roll and submitted the question whether we would then take the oath. This time almost all the Virginians said yes. Tom Watts, myself and four or five others from Virginia still held out.

When it became clear and undeniable that the Confederacy was defeated, some of the prisoners of war at Fort Delaware, like Dickinson, still refused to take the oath of allegiance to the victorious United States, though it was the only way to obtain release and return home. Randolph A. Shotwell, a prisoner from North Carolina, recorded General Schoepf's speech to the Confederate prisoners on May 2, 1865, when the commandant urged those who still refused to "swallow the yellow dog" to relent and take the oath of allegiance to the United States. After emphasizing that their Confederacy was "gone up and busted," the

"Dutchman" (as Shotwell called him) advised the "rebels" in his heavy foreign accent, "Git out, an' take allegiance to the pest government vat ever vas."

Of those who held out to the bitter end before taking the oath, a number were members of the surviving "Immortal 600." One of them, Captain George Nelson, wrote:

> *The fall of Richmond, Lee's surrender, and, finally, the capitulation of Johnston's army, soon swept away from us every hope of a Southern Confederacy. But one course remained, viz: swear allegiance to the Government in whose power we were. Upon doing this, I was released on the 13th of June, 1865.*

In his memoirs, Private George H. Moffett described his departure from Fort Delaware after sixteen months of incarceration there:

> *On the morning of the 20th of June, 1865, I was called out to the provost's office to subscribe to my "amnesty," and when this was performed I was told that I was again a free man. Strange as it may seem to the reader, the announcement of our release excited no enthusiasm among the freed prisoners. Possibly our long and miserable confinement had made us callous to events. All the buoyancy of youth was gone. At sixteen years of age I had quitted college to go into the war, and had just recently passed my twentieth birthday when released from Fort Delaware. I felt that the best period of my young manhood had been a wasted existence. Then again, we were men without a country…With that feeling of being aliens in a strange land, it is no wonder that our heartstrings should have been shadowed by solemn reflections.*
>
> *Within two hours of my release we were on a vessel steaming up the Delaware to Wilmington, where we took a train for Baltimore, to be again transferred to an old transport vessel which carried us down the Chesapeake to Fortress Monroe. Then another transfer to another steamer, which took us up the James River, landing us at Richmond in the afternoon of the third day.*
>
> *Back again in Dixie Land! But O how changed, and how different from what we had dreamed or hoped! It was a land of ruins.*

After the war, the prisoners who were released from Fort Delaware, like most ex-Confederates, struggled to earn a living and rebuild their lives and

A Confederate soldier returning home after the war. *From the collections of the South Carolina Historical Society.*

homes in "a land of ruins." John Ogden Murray paid the following tribute to these men:

> *We left sleeping in death at Fort Delaware some grand men—murdered by the cruelty of prison life. Those who lived through the ordeal returned to their homes to find them in ruins. Desolation had spread its black wings over our beloved South. The blue uniform of the Yankee soldier was to be seen everywhere. Yet, at the sight of all this ruin and desolation, the men who followed Lee did not falter. They went to work to rebuild, upon the ruins of the old, new homes. They soon convinced the world that they were as good builders as they were fighters. The same old courage, obedience, and fortitude that made them the ideal soldiers of the world came to their aid. From the wreck and the ruin of war was built the Southland of today; and built upon the only capital the Confederate soldier had after the war was done—his honor and courage.*

Afterword

Though little or nothing remains of wartime fortifications on Morris Island in Charleston Harbor or at Hilton Head Island, South Carolina, Fort Delaware survives largely intact as a state park, and Fort Pulaski, situated on the Georgia coast near Savannah, draws many visitors each year as a "national monument" operated by the National Park Service.

In 2011, a Sons of Confederate Veterans camp in Georgia obtained approval from the National Park Service to erect a monument to the Immortal 600 at Fort Pulaski, as well as a low perimeter wall to surround the site of the unmarked graves of the Confederate prisoners of war who were buried there. The project was completed in 2012, and in October of that year, a handsome stone monument was dedicated to honor and memorialize these men. It bears a bronze tablet listing the names, military units and the dates of death of the thirteen. The inscriptions on the stone include this eulogy to the six hundred:

BRAVE ON THE FIELD OF BATTLE
WITH STEADFAST LOYALTY TO COUNTRY AND COMRADES
THEY PLACED HONOUR ABOVE LIFE ITSELF

Visitors to Fort Pulaski will also read the following admonition, writ large across the base of the memorial:

LEST WE FORGET

A Note on Sources

One of the main sources consulted about conditions at Fort Delaware was Reverend Isaac W.K. Handy's diary, published in 1874 as *United States Bonds; or Duress by Federal Authority.* The principal sources about the experiences of the Immortal 600 were their memoirs and diaries that appeared in print after the war. Perhaps the most well known of these is John Ogden Murray's *The Immortal Six Hundred*, published in 1905. The prison diary of Captain Henry C. Dickinson was one of the most extensive accounts and the one used most extensively for this book. To date, the most authoritative and comprehensive work about the Immortal 600 is Mauriel P. Joslyn's outstanding book *Immortal Captives*, published in 1996. Louis F. Schade's letter of 1867 is found in the appendix of the book *Scraps from the Prison Table* by Joseph Barbiere, and the "Report of the Joint Committee of the Confederate Congress Appointed to Investigate the Condition and Treatment of Prisoners of War" was published in the *Southern Historical Society Papers* in 1876.

Bibliography

Barbiere, Joseph. *Scraps from the Prison Table, at Camp Chase and Johnson's Island.* Doyleston, PA: W.W.H. Davis, Printer, 1868.

Barnes, F.C., and R.E. Frayser. "Imprisoned Under Fire." *Southern Historical Society Papers* 25 (1897): 365–77.

Boynton, Charles B. *The History of the Navy During the Rebellion.* New York: D. Appleton and Company, 1868.

Calef, B.S. "Prison-Life in the Confederacy." *Harper's New Monthly Magazine* 31 (1865): 137–50.

Cook, Henry Howe. "The Story of the Six Hundred." *Confederate Veteran* 5 (n.d.): 116–18, 148–50, 219–20.

Dickinson, Henry Clay. *Diary of Captain Henry C. Dickinson, C.S.A.* Denver, CO: Williamson-Haffner Co., 1913.

Epps, William. "Diary," in *History of Williamsburg* by William Willis Boddie. Columbia, SC: State Company, 1923.

Evans, Clement A., ed. *Confederate Military History.* Atlanta, GA: Confederate Publishing Company, 1899.

Fulkerson, Abram. "The Prison Experience of a Confederate Soldier." *Southern Historical Society Papers* 22 (1894): 124–46.

Fuzzlebug, Fritz. *Prison Life During the Rebellion.* Singer's Glen, VA: J. Funk's Sons, 1869.

George, William W. *In a Federal Prison.* Baltimore, MD: King Printing Company, 1906.

Gillmore, Quincy A. *Official Report to the United States Engineer Department, of the Siege and Reduction of Fort Pulaski, Georgia.* New York: D. Van Nostrand, 1862.

Hamilton, J.G. De Roulhac, ed. *The Papers of Randolph Abbot Shotwell.* Raleigh: North Carolina Historical Commission, 1931.

Handerson, Henry E. *Yankee in Gray: The Civil War Memoirs of Henry E. Handerson.* Cleveland, OH: Press of Western Reserve University, 1962.

Handy, Isaac W.K. *United States Bonds; or Duress by Federal Authorities; A Journal of Current Events During an Imprisonment of Fifteen Months at Fort Delaware.* Baltimore, MD: Turnbull Brothers, 1874.

Hesseltine, William Best. "Atrocities, Then and Now." *The Progressive* 9 (1945): 4.

———. *Civil War Prisons: A Study in War Psychology.* Columbus: Ohio State University Press, 1930.

Johnson, John. *The Defense of Charleston Harbor: Including Fort Sumter and the Adjacent Islands, 1863–1865.* Charleston, SC: Walker, Evans & Cogswell Co., 1890.

Jones, Charles C. *Historical Sketch of the Chatham Artillery During the Confederate Struggle for Independence.* New York: Joel Munsell, 1867.

Jones, Samuel. *The Siege of Charleston, and the Operations on the South Atlantic Coast in the War Among the States.* New York: Neale Publishing Company, 1911.

Joslyn, Mauriel Phillips. *Immortal Captives: The Story of Six Hundred Confederate Officers and the United States Prisoner of War Policy.* Shippensburg, PA: White Mane Publishing, 1996.

LaBree, Ben, ed. *Camp Fires of the Confederacy.* Louisville, KY: Courier-Journal Job Printing Company, 1899.

Miller, Francis Trevelyan, ed. *The Photographic History of the Civil War. Vol. 7, Prisons and Hospitals.* New York: Review of Reviews Co., 1911.

Moffett, George H. "War Prison Experiences." *Confederate Veteran* 13 (1905): 105–10.

Murray, J. Ogden. *The Immortal Six Hundred.* Winchester, VA: Eddy Press, 1905.

O'Connor, Mary Doline. *The Life and Letters of M.P. O'Connor.* New York: Dempsey & Carroll, 1893.

Park, Robert E. "Diary of Capt. Park, 12th Alabama Regiment." *Southern Historical Society Papers* 3 (1877): 43–46, 55–61, 123–27, 183–89.

Phelps, W. Chris. *The Bombardment of Charleston, 1863–1865.* Gretna, LA: Pelican Publishing Company, 2002.

Pickenpaugh, Roger. *Captives in Gray: The Civil War Prisons of the Union.* Tuscaloosa: University of Alabama Press, 2009.

Ravenel, Harriott Horry. *Charleston, The Place and the People.* New York: Macmillan Company, 1912.

Roman, Alfred. *The Military Operations of General Beauregard in the War Between the States.* New York: Harper and Brothers, 1884.

Ross, Fitzgerald. *A Visit to Cities and Camps of the Confederate States.* London: W. Blackwood & Sons, 1865.

Sanders, Charles W. *While in the Hands of the Enemy: Military Prisons of the Civil War.* Baton Rouge: Louisiana State University Press, 2005.

Simms, William Gilmore, ed. *War Poetry of the South.* New York: Richardson & Company, 1867.

Speer, Lonnie. *Portals to Hell: Military Prisons of the Civil War.* Mechanicsburg, PA: Stackpole Books, 1997.

———. *War of Vengeance: Acts of Retaliation against Civil War POWs.* Mechanicsville, PA: Stackpole Books, 2002.

Tap, Bruce. *Over Lincoln's Shoulder: The Committee on the Conduct of the War.* Lawrence: University Press of Kansas, 1998.

Thomson, Jack. *Charleston at War: The Photographic Record 1860–1865.* Gettysburg, PA: Thomas Publications, 2000.

"Treatment of Prisoners." *Southern Historical Society Papers* 1 (1876): 112–62, 225–94.

United States Sanitary Commission. *Narrative of Privations and Sufferings of United States Officers and Soldiers While Prisoners of War in the Hands of the Rebel Authorities.* Philadelphia: King & Baird, 1864.

Warner, Ezra J. *Generals in Blue: Lives of the Union Commanders.* Baton Rouge: Louisiana State University Press, 1992.

GOVERNMENT RECORDS

War of the Rebellion: The Official Records of the Union and Confederate Armies. Washington, D.C.: Government Printing Office, 1880–1909.

MANUSCRIPTS AND ARCHIVAL SOURCES

SOUTH CAROLINA HISTORICAL SOCIETY:

Augustine Thomas Smythe Papers.

Bee-Chisolm Family Papers.

Harriott Horry Ravenel Family Papers.

Henry Wemyss Feilden Papers.

Pinckney, Thomas. "Reminiscences of the War and Reconstruction Times."

Porcher Family Papers.

WOFFORD COLLEGE LIBRARY SPECIAL COLLECTIONS:

W.E. Johnson Papers, The Littlejohn Collection.

Index

About the Author

K aren Stokes is an archivist with the South Carolina Historical Society in Charleston, South Carolina. She is a contributor to *The Civil War in South Carolina: Selections from the South Carolina Historical Magazine* and the co-editor of *Faith, Valor, and Devotion: The Civil War Letters of William Porcher DuBose* (2010) and *A Confederate Englishman: The Civil War Letters of Henry Wemyss Feilden*, released by the University of South Carolina Press in 2013. Her first book with The History Press, *South Carolina Civilians in Sherman's Path: Stories of Courage Amid Civil War Destruction*, was published in 2012.